Houghton Mifflin

Mathematics

Practice

2

HOUGHTON MIFFLIN BOSTON • MORRIS PLAINS, NJ

California • Colorado • Georgia • Illinois • New Jersey • Texas

Contents

Name ______________________ Date ____________

Add in Any Order

Find each sum.

1. 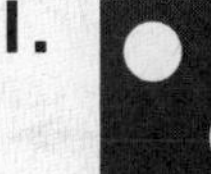 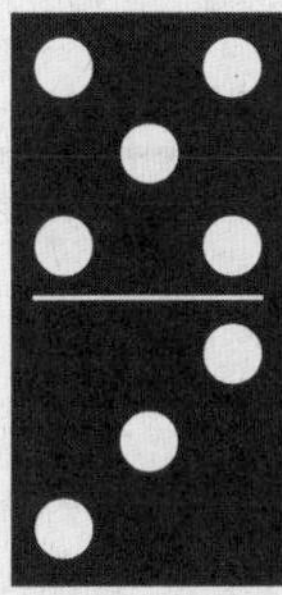

$\begin{array}{r} 5 \\ +3 \\ \hline 8 \end{array}$ $\begin{array}{r} 3 \\ +5 \\ \hline 8 \end{array}$

2. 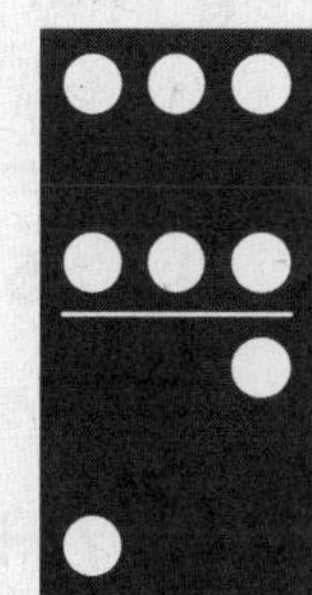

$\begin{array}{r} 6 \\ +2 \\ \hline \end{array}$ $\begin{array}{r} 2 \\ +6 \\ \hline \end{array}$

3. $\begin{array}{r} 7 \\ +0 \\ \hline \end{array}$ $\begin{array}{r} 0 \\ +7 \\ \hline \end{array}$

4. $\begin{array}{r} 4 \\ +2 \\ \hline \end{array}$ $\begin{array}{r} 2 \\ +4 \\ \hline \end{array}$

5. $\begin{array}{r} 3 \\ +2 \\ \hline \end{array}$ $\begin{array}{r} 2 \\ +3 \\ \hline \end{array}$

6. 5 + 4 = ____

   4 + 5 = ____

7. 10 + 0 = ____

   0 + 10 = ____

8. 6 + 1 = ____

   1 + 6 = ____

9. 9 + 1 = ____

   1 + 9 = ____

10. 2 + 7 = ____

    7 + 2 = ____

11. 8 + 2 = ____

    2 + 8 = ____

Problem Solving • Reasoning

Algebra Readiness • Number Sentences

Use what you know about adding in any order to find the missing numbers.

12. 5 + ____ = 0 + ____

13. 3 + ____ = 7 + ____

Name ____________________ Date __________

Count On to Add

Count on to add.
Use the number line to help you.

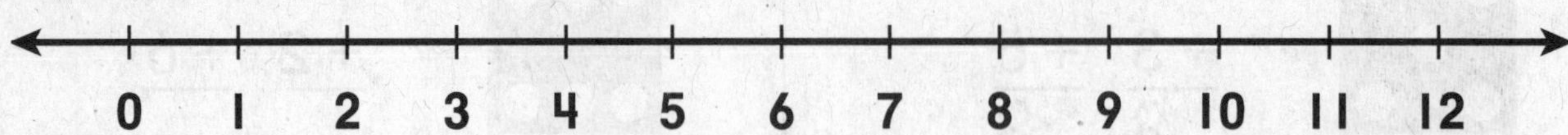

1. 4 + 2 = 6
2. 7 + 3 = ____
3. 3 + 5 = ____
4. ____ = 2 + 4
5. ____ = 8 + 3
6. ____ = 5 + 2

7. $\begin{array}{r} 6 \\ +3 \\ \hline \end{array}$
8. $\begin{array}{r} 1 \\ +2 \\ \hline \end{array}$
9. $\begin{array}{r} 2 \\ +8 \\ \hline \end{array}$
10. $\begin{array}{r} 2 \\ +7 \\ \hline \end{array}$

Problem Solving • Reasoning

11. Elise is baking 4 muffins today. Tomorrow she is going to bake 6 muffins. How many muffins will Elise bake altogether?

____ muffins

Draw or write to explain.

12. **Write Your Own** Write another story problem. Use a number line to help you. Then solve.

Name ______________________ Date ____________

Add Double Facts

Find each sum. Then circle the double facts.

1. $7 + 7 = 14$
2. $4 + 4$
3. $1 + 9$
4. $9 + 9$
5. $3 + 7$
6. $3 + 3$
7. $6 + 6$
8. $3 + 5$
9. $2 + 2 =$ ____
10. $7 + 6 =$ ____
11. $5 + 0 =$ ____
12. $5 + 5 =$ ____
13. $4 + 4 =$ ____
14. $9 + 3 =$ ____

Problem Solving • Reasoning

15. Julie has 6 flowers. She wants to give the same number of flowers to Juan and Sabrina on their birthdays. Draw how many flowers she will give each.

16. **Write About It** Tell how you solved Problem 15.

Name ______________________ Date ____________

Use Double Facts to Add

1. Complete the addition table.
Then circle the sums for the double facts.

+	0	1	2	3	4	5	6	7	8	9
0										
1			3		5					10
2										
3										
4										
5		6					11			
6										
7										
8										
9										

Problem Solving • Reasoning

Using Vocabulary

2. The sum of two numbers is 8. Write a number sentence to show what the two numbers could be.

____ + ____ = ____

Draw or write to explain.

Name ______________________ Date ____________

Add 10

Add. Use counters if you want.

1. 10 + 4 = 14
2. 3 + 10 = ____
3. 10 + 0 = ____
4. ____ = 10 + 5
5. ____ = 9 + 8
6. ____ = 10 + 9

7. 7 + 10 = ____
8. 10 + 8 = ____
9. 6 + 10 = ____
10. 0 + 10 = ____

11. 7 + 7 = ____
12. 5 + 10 = ____
13. 6 + 8 = ____
14. 10 + 1 = ____

15. 9 + 10 = ____
16. 4 + 10 = ____
17. 10 + 3 = ____
18. 6 + 4 = ____

Problem Solving • Reasoning

Algebra Readiness • Number Sentences

19. Start with a number and add 10. The sum is 15. What number did you start with? ____

20. A sum is 18. One addend is 8. What is the other addend? ____

Name ______________________ Date ____________

Make Ten to Add

Add. You can use paper clips or coins as counters.

1.	2.	3.	4.
$\begin{array}{r} 9 \\ +2 \\ \hline \end{array}$	$\begin{array}{r} 8 \\ +3 \\ \hline \end{array}$	$\begin{array}{r} 3 \\ +9 \\ \hline \end{array}$	$\begin{array}{r} 8 \\ +4 \\ \hline \end{array}$

5.	6.	7.	8.
$\begin{array}{r} 7 \\ +3 \\ \hline \end{array}$	$\begin{array}{r} 6 \\ +8 \\ \hline \end{array}$	$\begin{array}{r} 8 \\ +7 \\ \hline \end{array}$	$\begin{array}{r} 2 \\ +8 \\ \hline \end{array}$

Complete each addition sentence.

9.

Sums of 15
9 + ____ = 15
8 + 7 = ____
____ + 10 = 15

10.

Sums of 16
10 + 6 = ____
____ + 9 = 16
8 + ____ = 16

Problem Solving • Reasoning

Visual Thinking

Use the picture to solve the problem.

11. Gwen and Nick baked 11 cookies. They put some in a lunch box for their friends. How many cookies are in the lunch box?

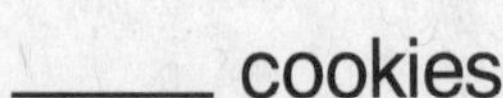

____ cookies

Draw or write to explain.

Name ______________________ Date ____________

Algebra Readiness:
Add Three Numbers

Find each sum.
Look for two numbers to add first.

1. $3 + 5 + 2 = 10$

2. $3 + 7 + 2$

3. $8 + 2 + 4$

4. $2 + 4 + 8$

5. $6 + 4 + 4$

6. $6 + 6 + 4$

7. $9 + 2 + 1$

8. $7 + 0 + 5$

9. 7 + 8 + 0 = ____

10. 9 + 2 + 2 = ____

11. 5 + 5 + 6 = ____

12. 6 + 7 + 6 = ____

Problem Solving • Reasoning

Algebra Readiness • Properties

Complete the number sentences.

13. Add these first.
3 + (7 + 2) = ?

3 + ____ = ____

Add these first.
(3 + 7) + 2 = ?

____ + 2 = ____

Name ______________________ Date ____________

Count Back to Subtract

Count back to subtract.
Use the number line to help you.

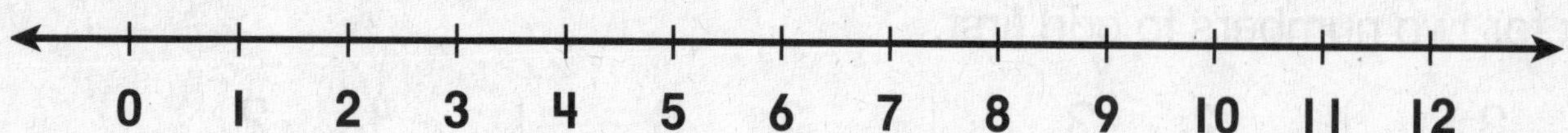

1. 7 − 2 = 5
2. 11 − 2 = ____
3. 9 − 3 = ____
4. 12 − 3 = ____
5. 8 − 3 = ____
6. 12 − 1 = ____

7. 11 − 3
8. 4 − 3
9. 10 − 2
10. 12 − 2

11. 9 − 2
12. 11 − 1
13. 10 − 3
14. 9 − 1

Problem Solving • Reasoning

Follow each rule.

15.

Add 2	
5	7
	8
9	
10	
	9

16.

Add 3	
	7
8	
	5
6	
	10

Name ______________________ Date ____________

Algebra Readiness:
Use Addition to Subtract

Add or subtract. Use cubes, blocks, or paper clips if you want.

1. 4 + 8 = 12

12 − 8 = 4

2. 5 + 2 = ____

7 − 2 = ____

3. 7 + 5 = ____

12 − 5 = ____

4. 9 + 3 = ____

12 − 3 = ____

5. 5 + 5 = ____

10 − 5 = ____

6. 4 + 3 = ____

7 − ____ = 4

7. 8 + 0 = ____

8 − 0 = ____

8. 1 + ____ = 11

11 − ____ = 10

Problem Solving • Reasoning

Write About It

2 4 6 7 8

9. Choose three of the numbers shown. Use the numbers to write two related facts.

____ + ____ = ____

____ − ____ = ____

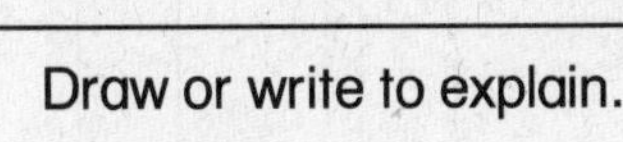

10. Explain why the facts are related.

Name ______________________________ Date ______________

Subtract From Numbers to 15

Use a paper clip and pencil. Spin the spinner two times. Use the numbers to write an addition fact. Then write two related subtraction facts.

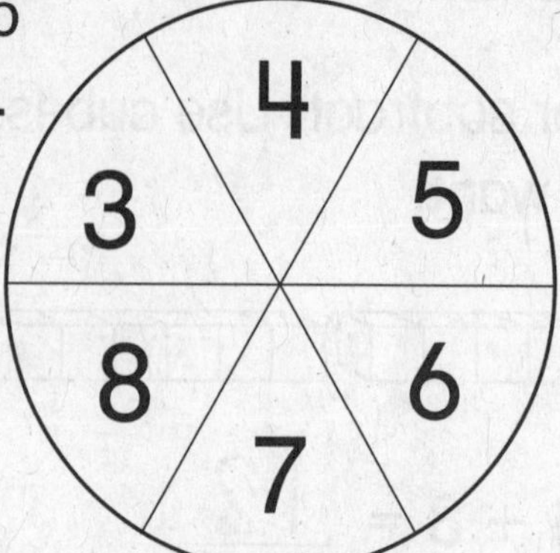

1. 8 + 4 = 12 12 − 4 = 8 12 − 8 = 4

2.

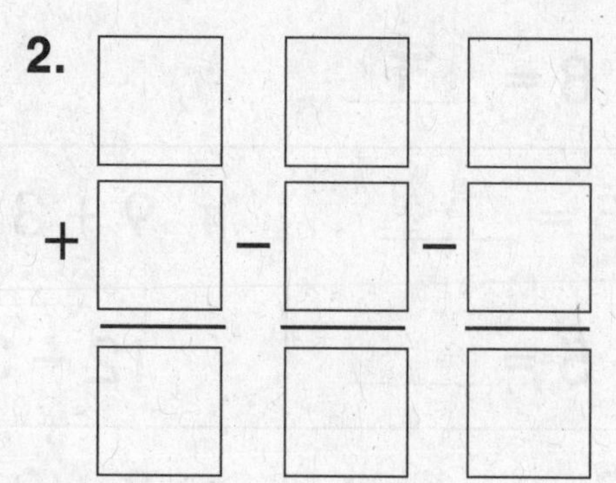

3.

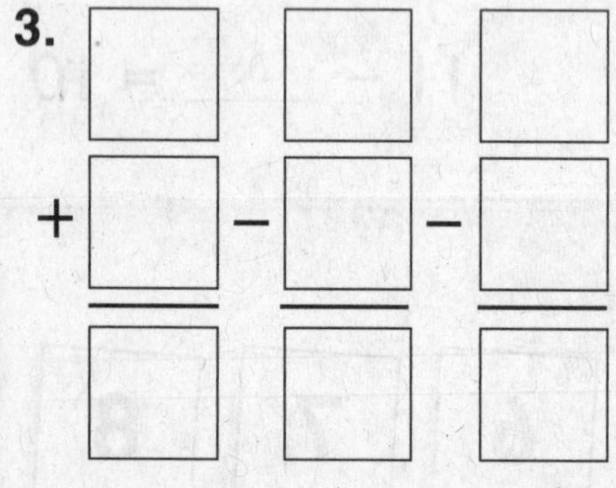

4.

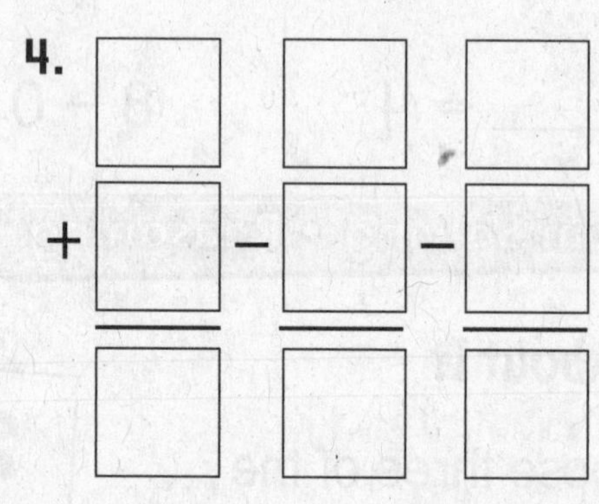

5.

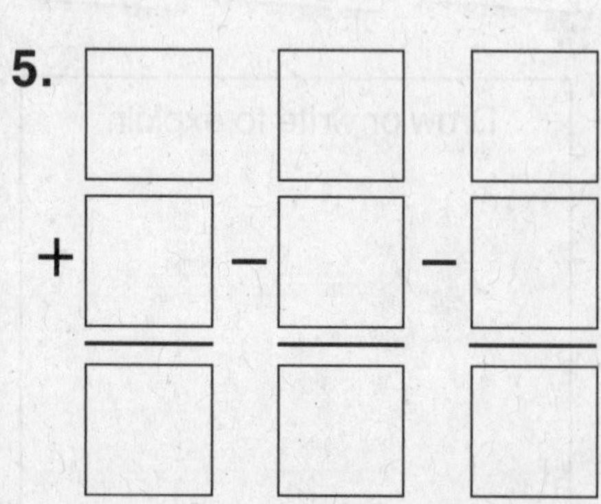

6.

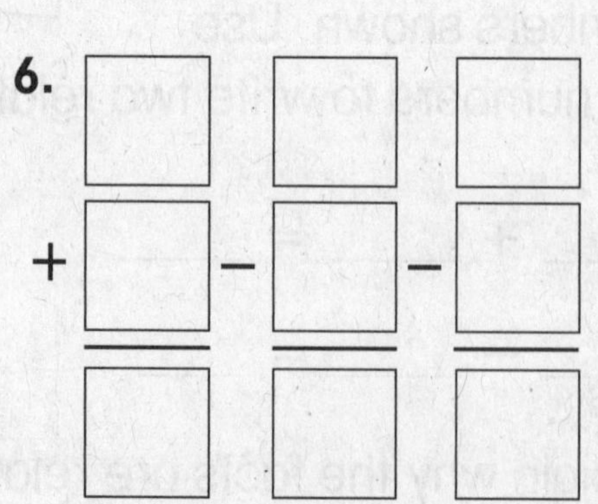

Name ______________________ Date ____________

Subtract From Numbers to 20

Add or subtract. Then match related facts.

1. 10 + 7 = 17 ⋯⋯ 17 − 7 = 10

1. 10 + 7 = 17	18 − 10 = ____
10 + 9 = ____	17 − 7 = 10
8 + 10 = ____	17 − 8 = ____
9 + 8 = ____	19 − 9 = ____
2. 9 + 9 = ____	18 − 9 = ____
9 + 7 = ____	15 − 7 = ____
7 + 8 = ____	20 − 9 = ____
9 + 11 = ____	16 − 7 = ____

Problem Solving • Reasoning

Write About It

3. Ned's score is 18. He tosses a beanbag three times and subtracts each number from his score. Now his score is 6. On which three numbers did the beanbag land?

9	7	0
2	6	1

____, ____, and ____

4. Explain how you know you are right.

Name ______________________ Date __________

Problem Solving: Write a Number Sentence

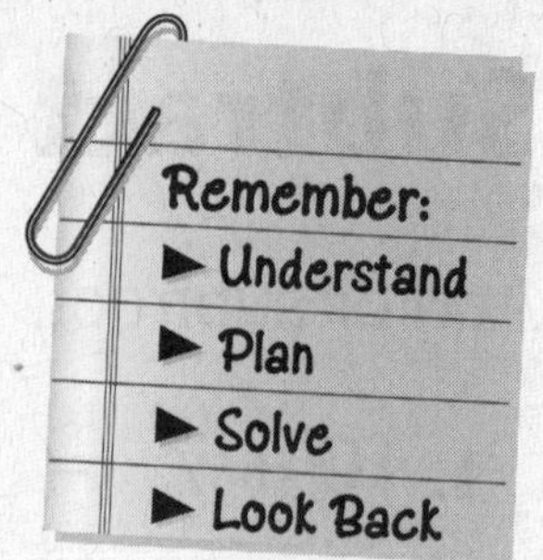

A number sentence can help you solve a problem.
Solve. Write each number sentence.

1. 6 frogs were on a lily pad. 5 frogs were on a log. How many frogs were there in all?

Think: What do I want to find out?

_____ + _____ = _____ frogs

Draw or write to explain.

---

2. 10 ducks were swimming on the pond. 3 flew away. How many ducks were left?

Think: What number do I start with?

_____ − _____ = _____ ducks

Draw or write to explain.

Solve. Choose a strategy.

- Draw a picture.
- Write a number sentence.

3. Ari has 8 worms. Amy has 7 worms. How many worms do they both have?

_____ + _____ = _____ worms

Draw or write to explain.

Name ______________________ Date __________

Subtract to Compare

Write each number sentence.
Use cubes, paper clips, or pennies if you want.

1. June sees 8 dolphins. Scott sees 6 dolphins. How many more dolphins does June see?

   8 – 6 = 2

2. Amy picks up 4 shells on the beach. Kerry picks up 9 shells. How many fewer shells does Amy pick up?

   ____ – ____ = ____

3. Holly sees 11 whales. Lee sees 7 whales. How many more whales does Lee see than Holly?

   ____ – ____ = ____

4. Mike catches 10 fish. Pat catches 12 fish. How many more fish does Pat catch than Mike?

   ____ – ____ = ____

Problem Solving • Reasoning

Using Data

Use the graph to solve the problem.

5. How many fewer gray shells than white shells are there? ____

6. How many white shells and black shells are there? ____

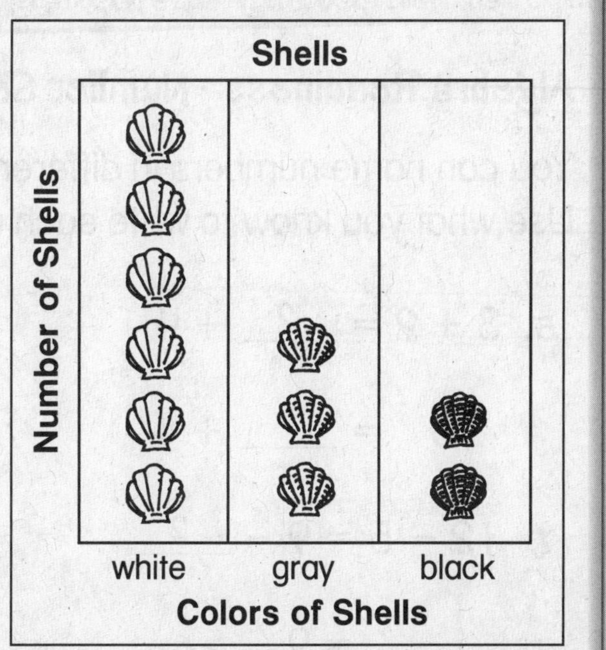

Name ______________________ Date __________

Algebra Readiness: Names for Numbers

Write addition and subtraction names for each number.

1. **4**   4 – 0   3 + 1   2 + 2

2. **9**   ____ – ____   ____ + ____   ____ – ____

3. **7**   ____ + ____   ____ + ____   ____ – ____

4. **6**   ____ + ____   ____ + ____   ____ – ____

Problem Solving • Reasoning

Algebra Readiness • Number Sentences

You can name numbers in different ways.
Use what you know to write each missing number.

5. 3 + 2 = ? + 4

   5 = ____ + 4

6. 3 + 5 = ? + 6

   ____ = ____ + 6

7. 12 – 5 = 9 – ?

   ____ = 9 – ____

8. 15 – ? = 8 + 2

   15 – ____ = ____

Name ______________________ Date ____________

Fact Families

Complete each number sentence.

1. 6 + 8 = 14
   8 + 6 = 14
   14 − 8 = 6
   14 − 6 = 8

2. 5 + 7 = ____
   7 + ____ = 12
   12 − 7 = ____
   12 − ____ = 7

3. 15 − 5 = ____
   ____ + 5 = 15
   ____ + 10 = 15
   15 − 10 = ____

4. ____ + 2 = 16
   16 − 14 = ____
   16 − ____ = 14
   ____ + 14 = 16

5. 18 − ____ = 8
   ____ + 8 = 18
   18 − 8 = ____
   8 + ____ = 18

6. 3 + 9 = ____
   ____ + 3 = 12
   ____ − 9 = 3
   12 − ____ = 9

Problem Solving • Reasoning

Logical Thinking

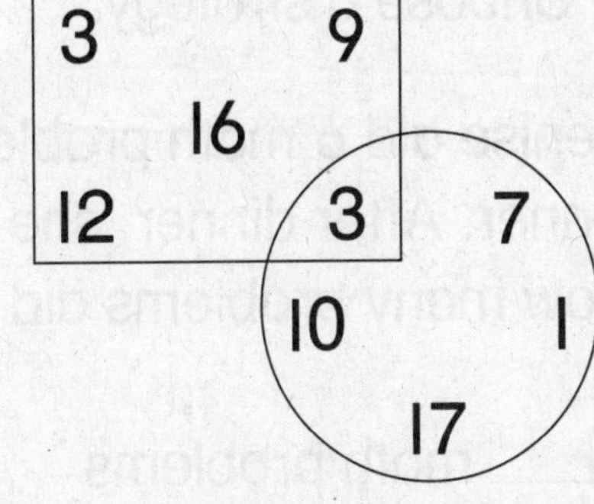

7. I am outside the circle. I am less than 15. You say my name when you count by 4s. ____

8. I am in the circle.
   I am the sum of two of the other numbers in the circle.
   I am more than 15. ____

Use with text pages 43–44.

Name ______________________ Date __________

Problem Solving: Choose the Operation

Sometimes you need to add or subtract to solve a problem.
Solve. Write each number sentence.

1. Marcus saw 7 ladybugs. Lisa saw 6 more. How many ladybugs did they both see?

Think: Do I need to add or subtract?

7 (+) 6 = 13 ladybugs

Draw or write to explain.

2. 11 children like carrots. 9 children like peas. How many more children like carrots than peas?

Think: What number do I start with?

____ ◯ ____ = ____ children

Draw or write to explain.

Solve. Choose a strategy.

- Draw a picture.
- Write a number sentence.

3. Denise did 6 math problems before dinner. After dinner, she did 4 more. How many problems did she do in all?

____ math problems

Draw or write to explain.

Name ____________________ Date __________

Tens to 100

Write the tens and ones. Write the number.

1. 7 tens

Tens	Ones
7	0

70

2. 3 tens

Tens	Ones

____

3. 6 tens

Tens	Ones

____

4. 2 tens

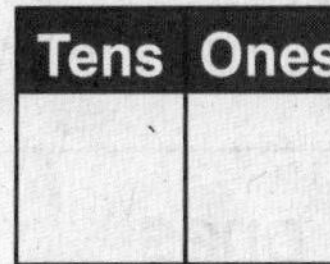

Tens	Ones

____

5. 8 tens

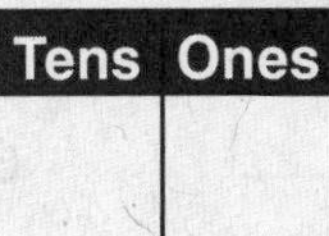

Tens	Ones

____

6. 1 ten

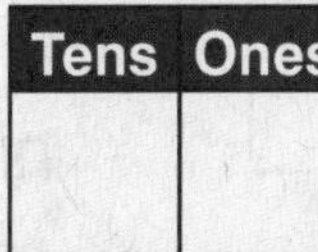

Tens	Ones

____

7. 5 tens

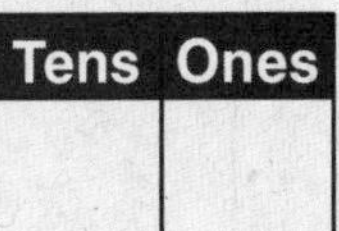

Tens	Ones

____

8. 9 tens

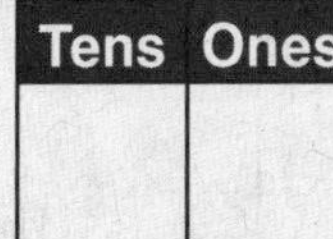

Tens	Ones

____

9. 1 ten

Tens	Ones

____

10. 4 tens

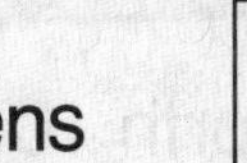

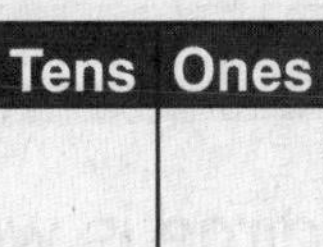

Tens	Ones

____

11. Write the missing numbers.

10, ____, 30, 40, ____, ____, 70, ____, 90, ____.

Problem Solving • Reasoning

12. How many 🍎 in all?

____ in all

Draw or write to explain.

Name ______________________ Date ____________

Tens and Ones to 100

Use a workmat with [tens block] and [ones block] if you want.
Write the tens and ones. Write the number.

1. 2 tens 4 ones

Tens	Ones
2	4

24
twenty-four

2. 4 tens 7 ones

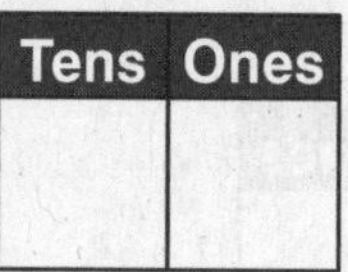

____
forty-seven

3. 9 tens 8 ones

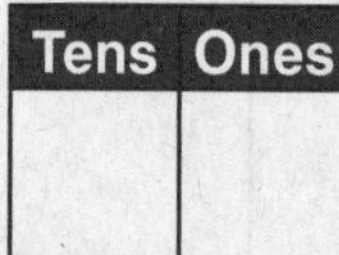

____
ninety-eight

4. 8 tens 9 ones

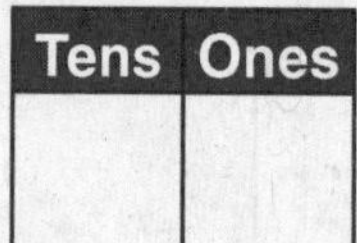

____
eighty-nine

5. 3 tens 3 ones

Tens	Ones

____
thirty-three

6. 6 tens 5 ones

Tens	Ones

____
sixty-five

Problem Solving • Reasoning

7. Each dime is worth 10¢.
Each nickel is worth 5¢.
Count the coins. Write how much.

Draw or write to explain.

____ ¢

____ ¢

____ ¢

____ ¢

____ ¢

____ ¢

Name ____________________ Date ____________

Identify Place Value

Write the numbers.

	How many tens and ones?	What is the value?	What is the number?
1. 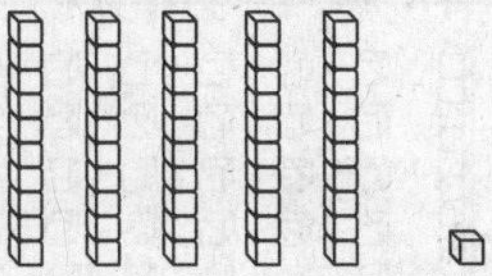	5 tens 1 ones	50 + 1	51
2. 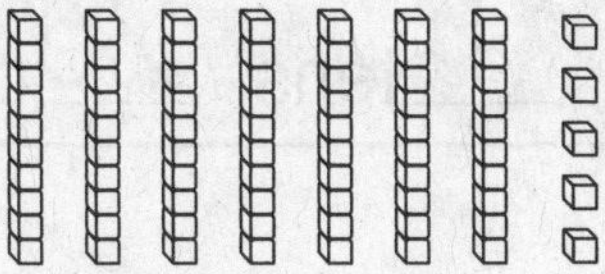	___ tens ___ ones	___ + ___	___
3. 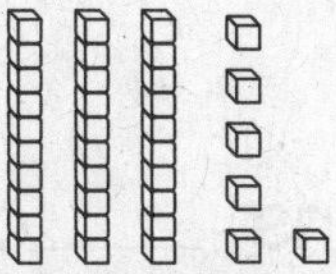	___ tens ___ ones	___ + ___	___
4. 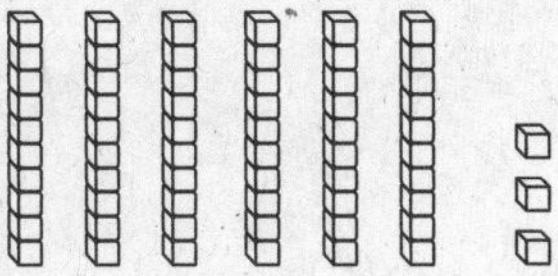	___ tens ___ ones	___ + ___	___
5. 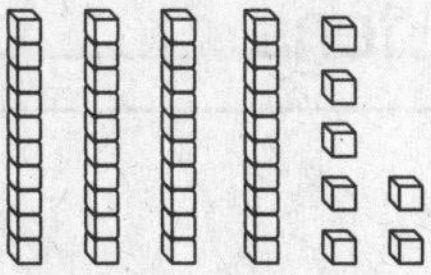	___ tens ___ ones	___ + ___	___

Problem Solving • Reasoning

6. I have one more tens than ones. The value of my ones digit is 8. What number am I?

______

Draw or write to explain.

7. **Write About It** Explain how you decided what number could be the answer.

Name ______________________ Date ____________

Regroup Tens as Ones

Use Workmat 3 with [tens block] and [ones block].

		Show the number of [tens block] and [ones block].	Regroup 1 ten as 10 ones. Record.	Regroup another ten as 10 ones. Record.
1.	36		2 tens 16 ones	1 tens 26 ones
2.	53		____ tens ____ ones	____ tens ____ ones
3.	44		____ tens ____ ones	____ tens ____ ones

Problem Solving • Reasoning

Write About It

4. Write the number of tens and ones blocks. **Explain** how you could regroup the tens and ones blocks to show the number in another way. Write how many tens and ones you have.

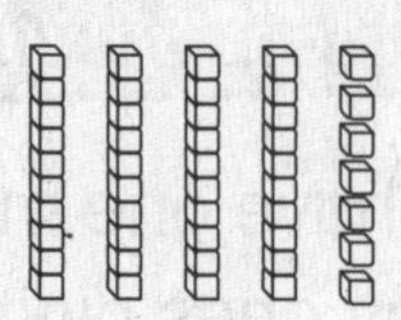

____ tens ____ ones

____ tens ____ ones

Name ______________________ Date ____________

Different Ways to Show Numbers

Write each number.

1. = 45

2. 20 + 9 = ____ 

3. 8 tens 7 ones = ____

4.  = ____

5. = ____

6. 9 tens 9 ones = ____

7. 40 + 6 = ____

8. 5 tens and 1 one = ____

Problem Solving • Reasoning

Number Sense

9. You have these tens and ones models.

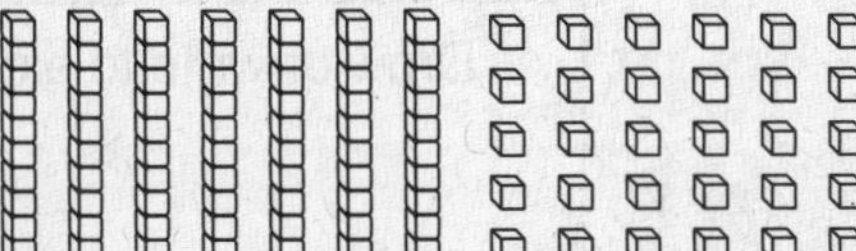

How many tens and ones would you use to show 84? ____ tens blocks ____ ones blocks

Name ______________________ Date __________

Problem Solving: Too Much Information

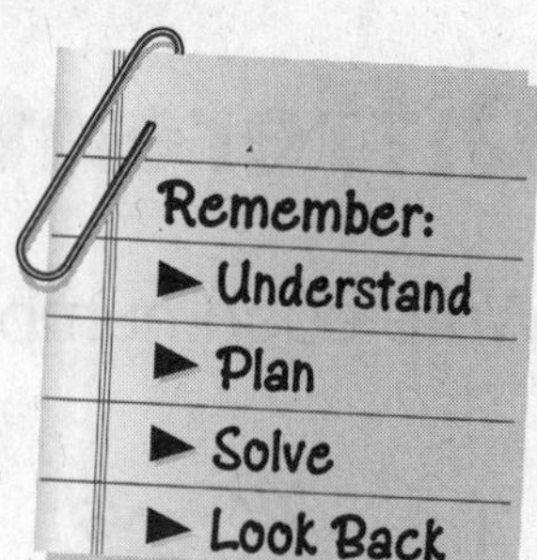

Sometimes a problem has information that you do not need. Cross out the information you do not need. Then solve.

1. Marvin the Great pulled 12 birds out of his hat. Then he pulled 8 flowers out of his hat. After that, he pulled 6 rabbits out of his hat. Did he pull out more rabbits or more birds?

   Think: Can I cross out any information?

   Draw or write to explain.

   He pulled more ________ out of the hat.

2. Our team won 7 blue ribbons, 8 red ribbons, and 5 green ribbons. Then we won 4 more blue ribbons. How many blue ribbons did we win in all?

   Think: Do I add or subtract?

   Draw or write to explain.

   _____ blue ribbons

Solve. Choose a strategy.

- Draw a picture.
- Write a number sentence.

3. Lily has 8 toy horses. She also has 3 teddy bears. If she gets 2 more toy horses, how many will she have?

   Draw or write to explain.

   _____ toy horses

Name ______________________ Date ______________

Even and Odd Numbers

Show each number with cubes.
Then circle even or odd.

1. 9 even odd

2. 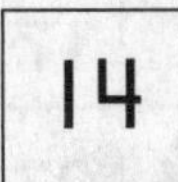 14 even odd

3. 23 even odd

4.  5 even odd

5. 6 even odd

6. 22 even odd

7. 28 even odd

8. 25 even odd

Problem Solving • Reasoning

9. Color the even numbers Red. Color the odd numbers Blue.

21	22	23	24	25	26	27	28	29	30
31	32	33	34	35	36	37	38	39	40

10. Write the next even number ____.

Write the next odd number ____.

Name ______________________________ Date ______________

Number Patterns

1. Write the missing numbers in the hundred chart.

1		3	4	5		7		9	
11	12			15		17			20
	22		24		26	27			
31			34	35				39	40
	42		44		46			49	
51		53		55		57			
61		63				67		69	70
71			74	75		77			80
	82		84		86			89	
91		93		95		97	98		100

Use the hundred chart to complete the pattern.

2. 3, 6, 9, ____, 15, ____, ____, ____, 27, 30

3. 32, 34, 36, ____, 40, ____, ____, ____, 48, ____

Problem Solving • Reasoning

Visual Thinking

4. Monica made this pattern. How should the last three circles be colored to continue the pattern? Circle the answer.

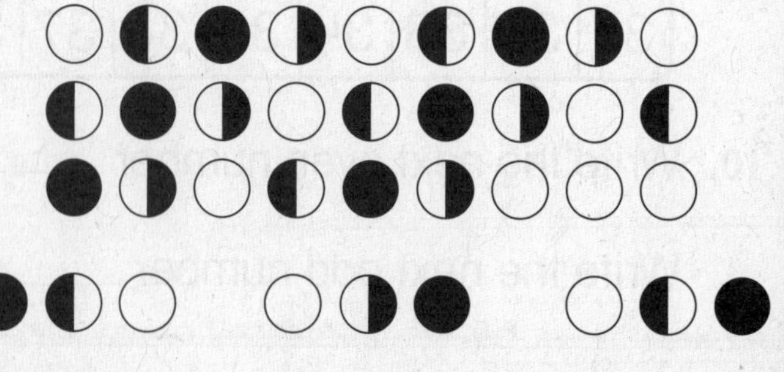

Name ______________________ Date ____________

Compare Two-Digit Numbers

Compare the numbers. Write >, <, or = in the ◯.

1. 68 (>) 65
2. 30 ◯ 86
3. 54 ◯ 77
4. 42 ◯ 15
5. 19 ◯ 19
6. 50 ◯ 38
7. 86 ◯ 35
8. 41 ◯ 41
9. 72 ◯ 91
10. 24 ◯ 22
11. 66 ◯ 99
12. 21 ◯ 12

Problem Solving • Reasoning

13. Jan has 4 tens and 3 ones. Sue has 3 tens and 4 ones. Who has the greater amount?

____

14. Did you compare the tens values or the ones values to find the answers above? Circle your answer.

Tens Ones

15. Marco has 6 tens cubes and 8 ones cubes. Tomas has 68 ones cubes. Circle the sentence that is correct.

A. Marco has more cubes.
B. Tomas has more cubes.
C. Marco and Tomas have the same number of cubes.

Name ______________________ Date __________

Order Two-Digit Numbers

Use each number line. Write the numbers.

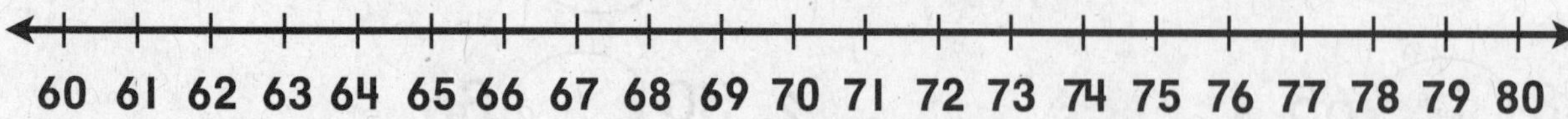

	Just Before	Between	Just After
1.	____, 66	67, ____, 69	68, ____
2.	____, 71	70, ____, 72	73, ____
3.	____, 80	61, ____, 63	60, ____

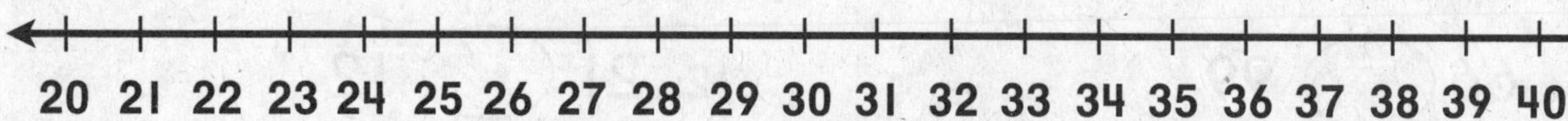

4. What number is just before 35? ____
5. What number is between 27 and 29? ____
6. What number is just after 39? ____
7. 27, 28, ____, ____, 31, ____, 33, 34, ____, 36, ____
8. 30, 29, 28, ____, ____, 25, ____, 23, ____, ____, 20

Problem Solving • Reasoning

Logical Thinking

9. A number is between 59 and 62. It has no ones. What is the number? ____

10. A number is between 10 and 15. It has the same number of tens and ones. What is it? ____

 Use with text pages 87–88.

Name ______________________________ Date ______________

Round to the Nearest Ten

Use the number line. Round each number to the nearest ten.

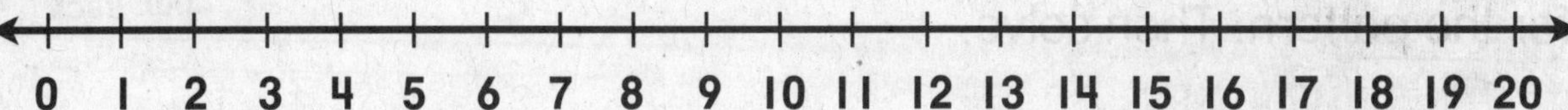

1. 16 rounds to 20.
2. 11 rounds to _____.
3. 7 rounds to _____.
4. 13 rounds to _____.
5. 19 rounds to _____.
6. 8 rounds to _____.

70 71 72 73 74 75 76 77 78 79 80 81 82 83 84 85 86 87 88 89 90

7. 78 rounds to _____.
8. 82 rounds to _____.
9. 89 rounds to _____.
10. 74 rounds to _____.

Problem Solving • Reasoning

Logical Thinking

11. A number is between 10 and 20. It rounds to 20. One of this number's digits is 5 greater than the other. What number is it? _____

Draw or write to explain.

Name ______________________ Date ____________

Problem Solving: Find a Pattern

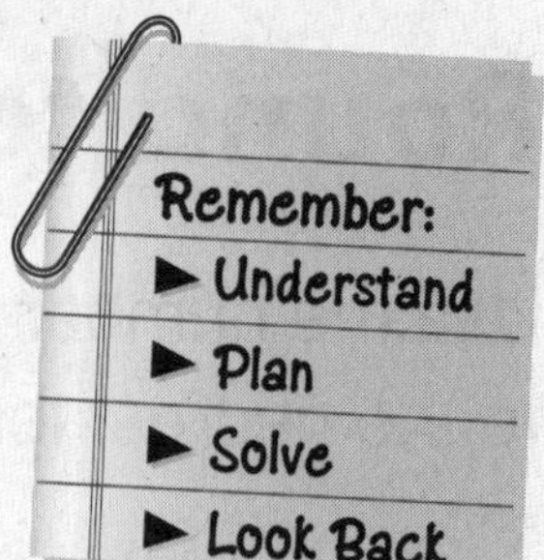

Sometimes you can find a pattern to solve a problem. Look for the pattern. Then solve.

1. Each dog eats 3 bones. How many bones will 5 dogs eat?

Think: What numbers do I already know?

Dogs	1	2	3	4	5
Bones	3	6	9		

_____ bones

2. Each pencil costs 5¢. How much do 6 pencils cost?

Think: What is the pattern?

Pencils	1	2	3	4	5	6
Cents	5	10	15			

_____¢ cents

Solve. Choose a strategy.

- Draw a picture.
- Write a number sentence.

3. There are 2 blue birds in each cage. How many blue birds are in 4 cages?

_____ blue birds

Draw or write to explain.

4. Julio made 19 pancakes. His brothers ate 9 of them. How many were left?

_____ pancakes

Draw or write to explain.

Name ______________________________ Date ______________

Make a Tally

1. Make a tally mark for each ball.
   Write the total.

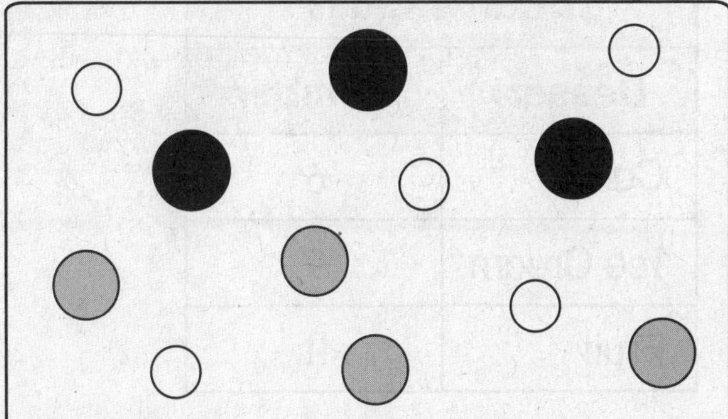

Ball	Tally	Total
(gray ball)	||||	4
(white ball)		____
(black ball)		____

Use the table to answer each question.

2. How many  are there?

   ____

3. 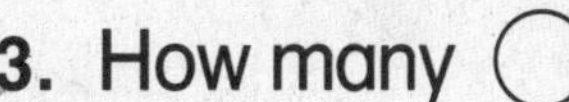 How many ○ are there?

   ____

4. How many more ○ than  are there?

   ____

5. How many balls are there altogether?

   ____

Problem Solving • Reasoning

6. Help Doria count these tally marks.

   ____, ____, ____, ____

7. This is Eve's count of tally marks: 5, 10, 11, 12, 13. Draw the tally marks she counts.

   ____

Name ____________________ Date ____________

Compare Data in Tables

These are the children's favorite desserts.
Use both tables to answer each question.

Erin's Class	
Dessert	**Number**
Cake	8
Ice Cream	6
Fruit	9

Brian's Class	
Dessert	**Number**
Cake	6
Ice Cream	9
Fruit	4

1. In whose class do more children like cake best?

   Erin's class

2. In whose class do more children like ice cream best?

   ________ class

3. How many children voted for fruit in both classes?

   _____ children

4. How many children voted for cake in both classes?

   _____ children

Problem Solving • Reasoning

5. Use the clues to complete the table.
   - There are 5 oranges.
   - There are 3 fewer bananas than oranges.
   - The number of apples and grapes is the same.
   - There are 13 fruits in all.

Fruit	Number
Oranges	
Apples	
Bananas	
Grapes	

Name ______________________ Date __________

Read a Pictograph

The table shows how many shirts of each color are in the store window.

Shirts			
Blue	Green	Red	White
4	6	10	8

1. Use the table to make a pictograph. Draw 1 △ for every 2 shirts.

Shirts	
Blue	△ △
Green	
Red	
White	

Each △ stands for 2 shirts.

Use the pictograph to answer the questions.

2. How many more shirts are red than green?

_____ more shirts

3. If 2 more white shirts are added, how many △ will you add to the pictograph? _____ △

Problem Solving • Reasoning

Use the pictograph.

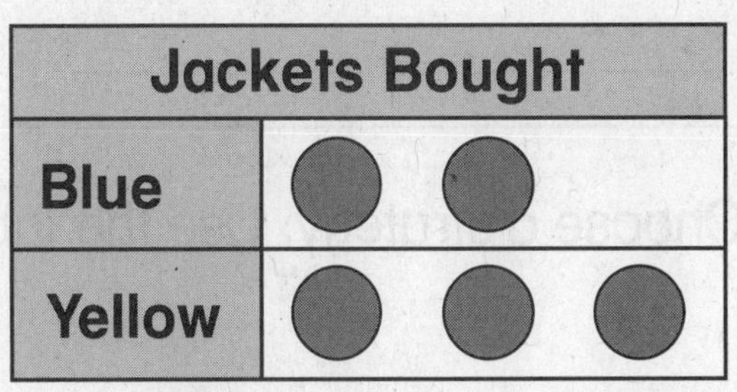

Jackets Bought	
Blue	● ●
Yellow	● ● ●

Each ● stands for 4 jackets.

4. How many blue jackets were bought?

_____ blue jackets

5. **Write About It** Explain how you counted the number of jackets.

Name ______________________ Date ____________

Problem Solving: Use Logical Thinking

Remember:
- ▶ Understand
- ▶ Plan
- ▶ Solve
- ▶ Look Back

You can use clues to solve a problem.

Use the table. Solve.

Favorite Field Trip	
Trips	**Number of Votes**
Zoo	12
Museum	7
Beach	16
Farm	8

1. Lisa's favorite trip got more than 10 votes, but did not get the most number of votes. What trip did Lisa like?

   Think: Which trip got the most votes?

   ____

2. Roberto's favorite trip got less than 12 votes. It got an even number of votes. What trip did Roberto like?

   Think: Which trips got an even number of votes?

   ____

   Draw or write to explain.

Solve. Choose a strategy. Use the table.

- Draw a picture.
- Use logical thinking.
- Use models to act it out.

3. How many more people like the beach than the musem?

   _____ people

4. How many votes did the farm and the museum get altogether?

   _____ votes

Name ______________________ Date ____________

Read a Bar Graph

Use the bar graph to answer each question.

1. How many children chose the beach?

 5 children

2. How many more children chose the beach than the lake?

 _____ children

3. How many more children chose the amusement park than the lake?

 _____ children

4. How many children chose the beach and the amusement park?

 _____ children

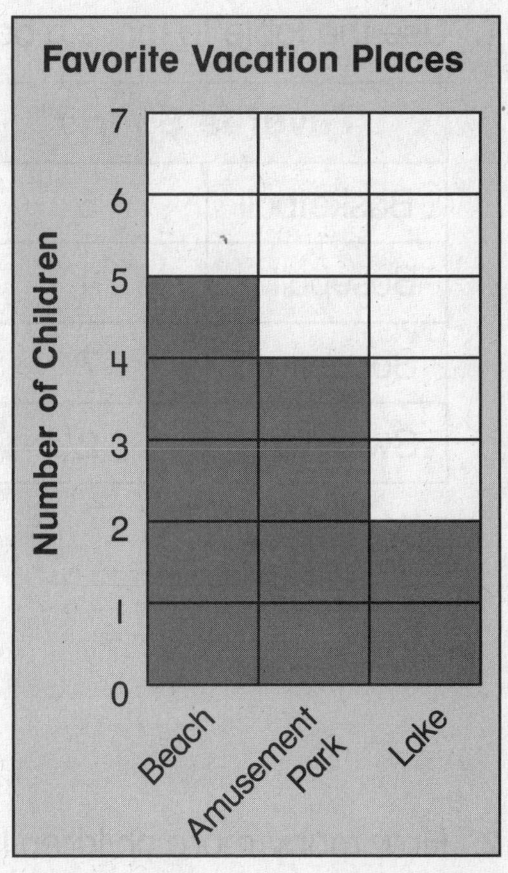

Problem Solving • Reasoning

Use the bar graph.

5. How many children like swimming?

 _____ children

6. **Write Your Own** Use the graph to write your own problem. Then solve.

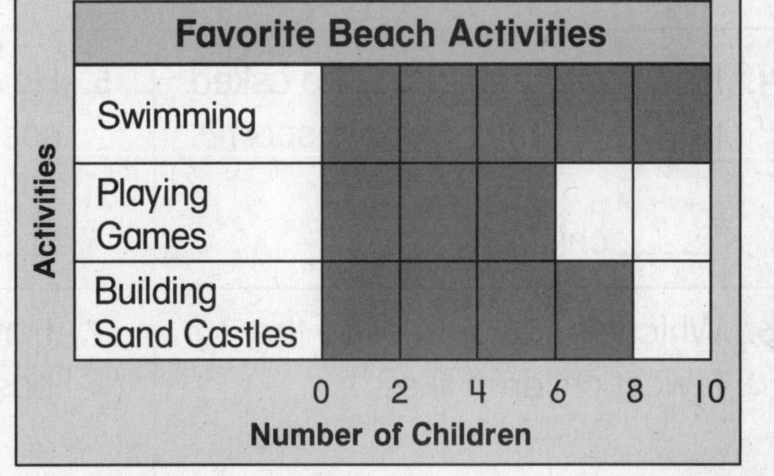

Name ______________________ Date __________

Make a Bar Graph

1. Use the table to make a bar graph.

Favorite Sports	
Basketball	5
Baseball	4
Soccer	7
Swimming	2

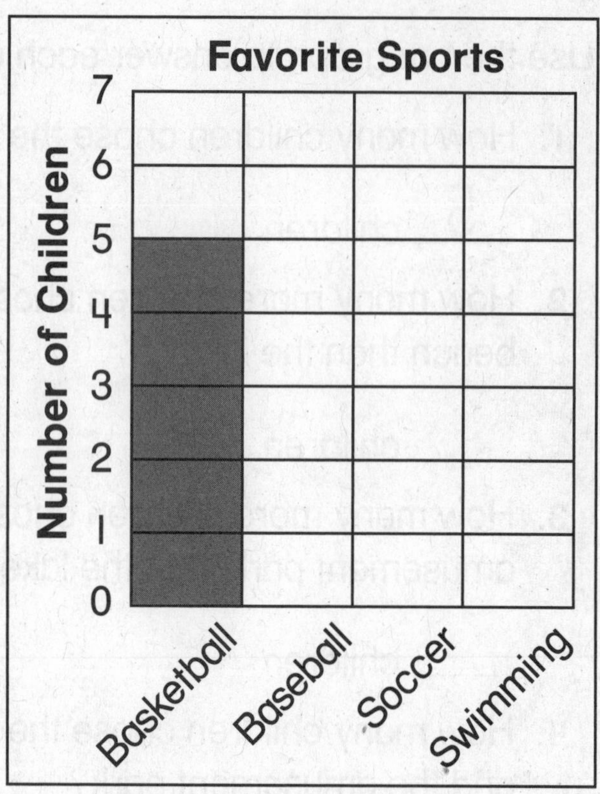

2. How many more children like soccer than baseball?

_____ children

3. How many children like soccer the most?

_____ children

4. How many children were asked to vote for their favorite sport?

_____ children

5. How many more children like soccer than swimming?

_____ children

6. Which sports activity do the fewest children like?

____

7. How many children like baseball and soccer?

_____ children

Name ______________________ Date ____________

Range and Mode

Use the information to answer each question.

Bike Rides in a Week	Number of Children
1	//
2	/
3	~~////~~
4	/
5	////

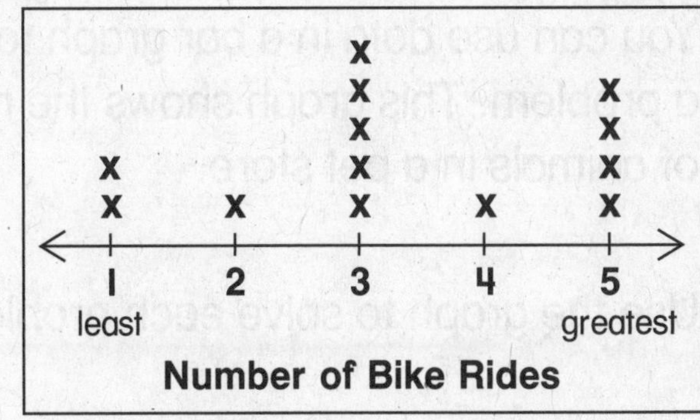

1. How many children rode one time?

   2 children

2. How many children rode three times?

   _____ children

3. Which number of bike rides has the greatest number of x's?

   _____ mode

4. What is the difference between the greatest number of rides and the least number of rides?

   _____ − _____ = _____
   greatest least range

Problem Solving • Reasoning

5. Make a bar graph to show the same data as the pictograph.

Movies Seen	
Juan	● ● ● ●
Ruby	● ●

Each ● stands for 4 movies.

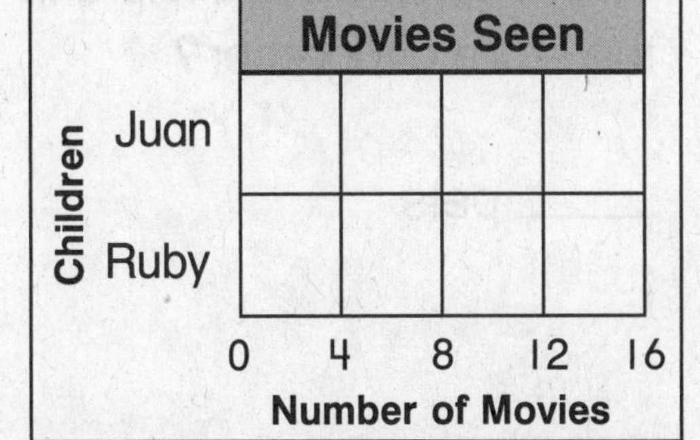

Name ______________________ Date __________

Problem Solving: Use a Graph

You can use data in a bar graph to solve a problem. This graph shows the number of animals in a pet store.

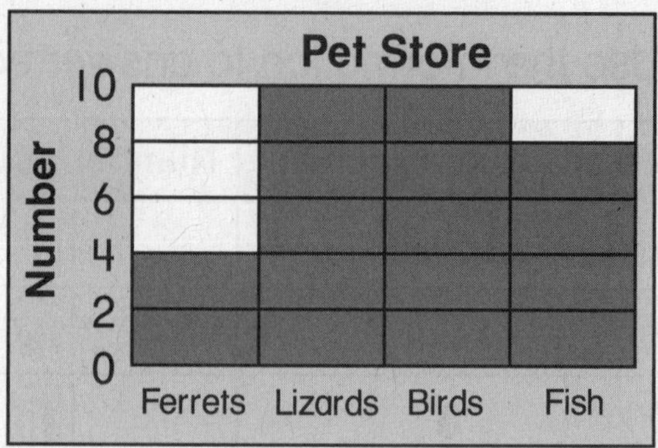

Use the graph to solve each problem.

1. How many birds are there in the pet store?

   _____ birds

   Think: How do I use the graph to answer the question?

   Draw or write to explain.

2. How many more lizards than ferrets are there?

   _____ more lizards

   Think: Which numbers do I use?

   Draw or write to explain.

Solve. Choose a strategy. Use the graph.

- Use a table.
- Use models to act it out.
- Write a number sentence.

3. How many pets are there in the store altogether?

   _____ pets

4. Oh no! 2 of the birds flew away! How many birds are left?

   _____ birds

Name ______________________ Date ______________

Dimes, Nickels, and Pennies

Write the total value of the coins.

1.     

10¢ 20¢ 25¢ 30¢ 35¢ 36¢

Total 36¢

2.     

____¢ ____¢ ____¢ ____¢ ____¢

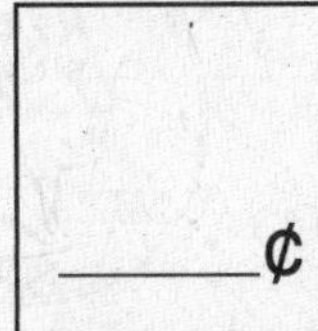

Total ____¢

3.     

____¢ ____¢ ____¢ ____¢ ____¢

Total ____¢

Problem Solving • Reasoning

4. When I buy popcorn I count my money like this: 5¢, 15¢, 25¢, 35¢, 45¢, 46¢. How many of each coin do I have?

____ dimes ____ nickel ____ penny

Name ______________________ Date ____________

Quarter, Dimes, and Nickels

Write the total value of the coins.

1.    

25 ¢ 35 ¢ 45 ¢ 55 ¢ 60 ¢

Total

60 ¢

2.  

_____ ¢ _____ ¢ _____ ¢ _____ ¢

Total

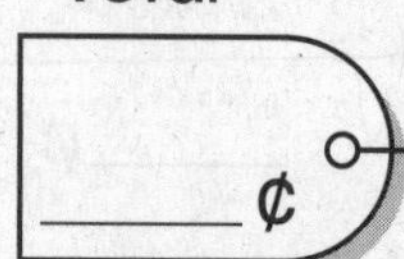

_____ ¢

3.   

_____ ¢ _____ ¢ _____ ¢ _____ ¢ _____ ¢

Total

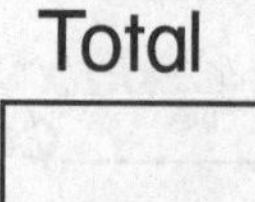

_____ ¢

Problem Solving • Reasoning

4. I have two coins that total 30¢.
   How many of each coin do I have?

   _____ quarter _____ dimes _____ nickel

5. **Write About It** Explain how you found your answer.

Name ______________________ Date ____________

Count Coins

Count the coins. Write the total amount.

1. 

61 ¢

2. 

_____ ¢

3. 

_____ ¢

4. 

_____ ¢

5. 

_____ ¢

6. 

_____ ¢

Problem Solving • Reasoning

7. I have 3 quarters, 1 dime, and 4 pennies.

   How much do I have? _____ ¢

8. I have 2 quarters. My friend has 6 dimes.

   How much do I have? _____ ¢

   How much does my friend have? _____ ¢

   Circle the greater amount.

Name ______________________________ Date ______________

Equal Amounts

Use coins. Show two ways to make each amount. Draw the coins.

1. 42¢	42¢
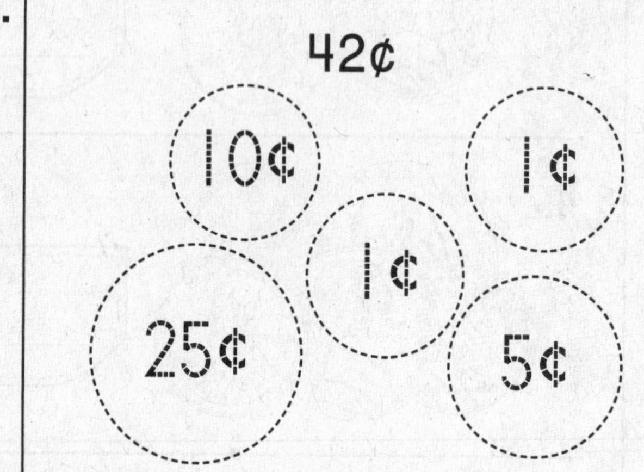	

2. 30¢	30¢

Problem Solving • Reasoning

3. You have 2 quarters. What other combinations of coins could you use to have the same amount?

____

Name ______________________ Date ______________

Compare Money Amounts

Write the total value of each group of coins.
Compare. Write >, <, or = in the ◯.

1. 

35 ¢ (=) 35 ¢

2. 

_____ ¢ ◯ _____ ¢

3. 

_____ ¢ ◯ _____ ¢

Problem Solving • Reasoning

4. Jill wants to buy a doll that costs 52¢.
She has 1 quarter and 2 dimes.
Does Jill have enough to buy the doll?

____

Draw or write to explain.

Name ______________________ Date __________

Problem Solving: Use Models to Act It Out

Remember:
- ► Understand
- ► Plan
- ► Solve
- ► Look Back

Sometimes you can use coins to help you solve problems. Solve. Use coins if you need to.

1. Anna has 4 dimes and 2 nickels. If she loses 1 dime, how much will she have left?

   Think: How much money did she start with?

   ______¢

   Draw or write to explain.

2. Sasha has 2 quarters and 5 pennies. An ice-cream cone costs 75¢. How much more money does he need to buy an ice-cream cone?

   Think: What coins does he need to make 75¢?

   ______¢

   Draw or write to explain.

Solve. Choose a strategy.

- Draw a picture.
- Use models to act it out.

3. Alice wants a book that costs 90¢. She has 5 dimes and 1 quarter. How much more does she need?

   ______¢

   Draw or write to explain.

Name ______________________________ Date ______________

Half-Dollars

Write the total value of the coins.

1. 

85 ¢

2. 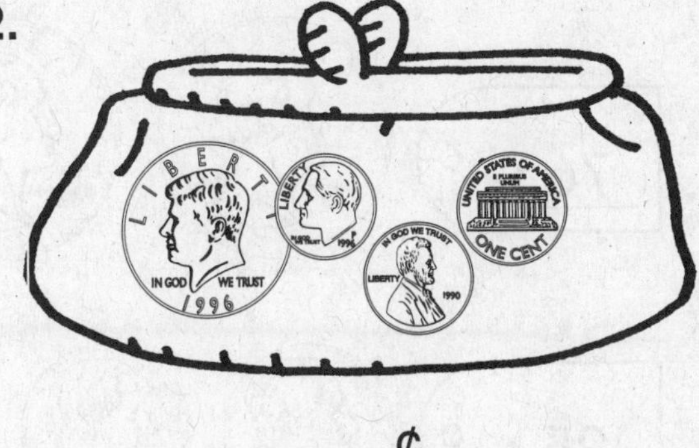

_____ ¢

3. 

_____ ¢

4. 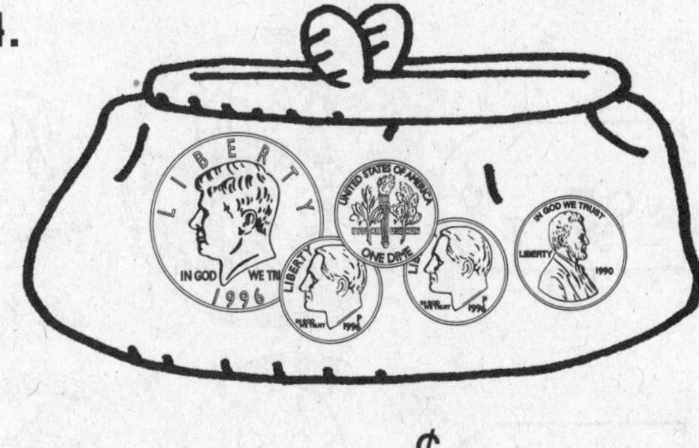

_____ ¢

5. 

_____ ¢

6. 

_____ ¢

Problem Solving • Reasoning

7. Circle the change purse with the least amount.

8. Write the greatest amount. _____ ¢

Name ______________________ Date __________

Use Money

Pay the exact amount. Draw a line to the coin you need from the bank.

1. 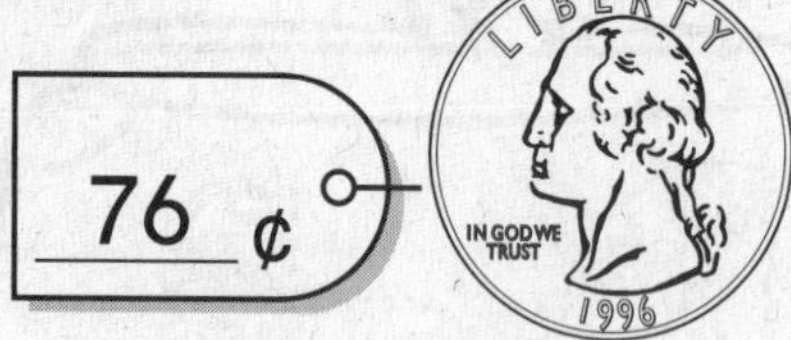

2. 

3. 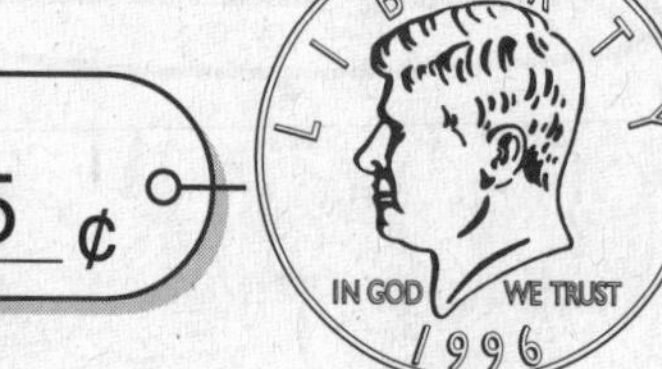

4. 

Problem Solving • Reasoning

5. You have 4 coins that equal the exact amount you need to buy a bag of peanuts. Draw the coins that you have.

Draw or write to explain.

Name ______________________ Date ____________

Use Coins to Show an Amount

Show each amount with coins. Use coins of the greatest value. Write how many of each coin.

1.

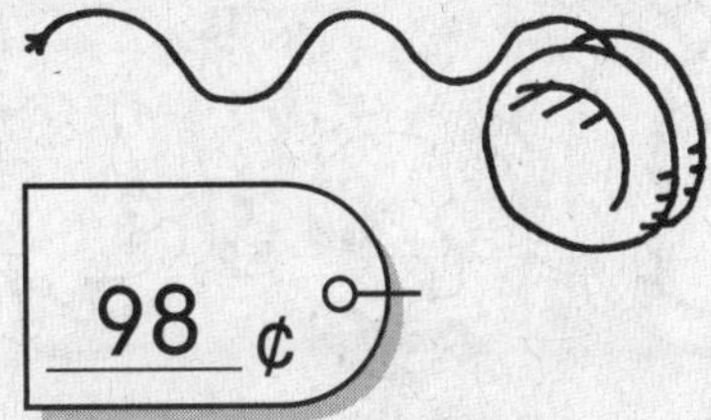

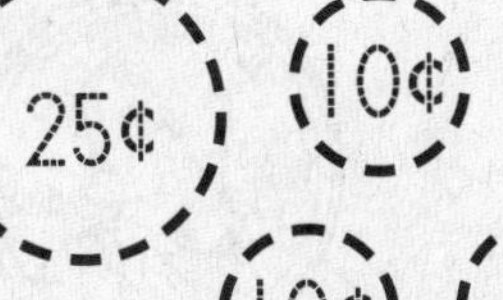

2.

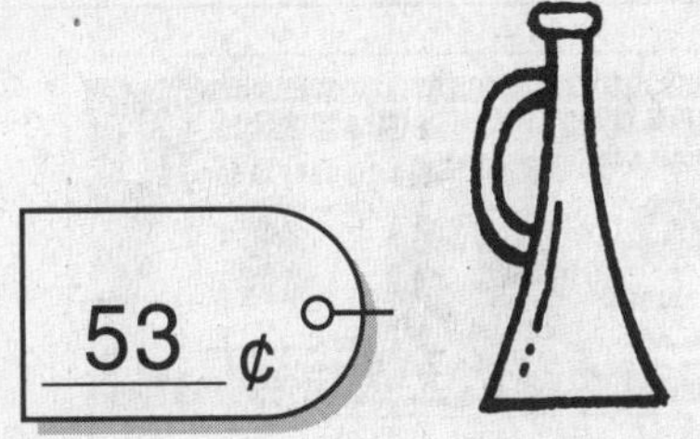

3.

Problem Solving • Reasoning

Erin and Matt both get 75¢ from their parents. Draw the coins that each child has.

4. Erin has 4 coins.

Draw or write to explain.

5. Matt has 2 coins.

Draw or write to explain.

Name ______________________________ Date ______________

One Dollar

Write each total amount. Circle the groups of coins that equal one dollar.

1.

_____¢

2.

_____¢

3.

_____¢

4.

_____¢

5.

_____¢

6.

_____¢

Problem Solving • Reasoning

7. Jill has $1.00 and Mike has 100¢. Who has more?

____

8. Explain your answer.

____

Name ______________________ Date __________

Make Change

Write the amount paid. Count on from the price to find the change.

Price	Amount Paid	Change
1. 43¢	45 ¢	2 ¢
2. 73¢	____ ¢	____ ¢
3. 57¢	____ ¢	____ ¢

Problem Solving • Reasoning

97¢

4. Anna pays for her book with 2 half-dollars. How much change will she get?

____ ¢

Draw or write to explain.

Name ______________________ Date ____________

Problem Solving: Multistep Problems

Sometimes you need more than one step to solve a problem.

Solve. Use coins if you need to.

1. Carla has 2 quarters and 2 nickels. She buys an apple for 20¢ and milk for 30¢. How much money does Carla have?

   Think: Do I add or subtract 20¢? Do I add or subtract 30¢?

   Draw or write to explain.

   Carla has _____¢.

2. Toshi has 35¢. He finds 1 quarter and 2 nickels when he sweeps the floor. How much money does he have now?

   Think: What should I do first?

   Draw or write to explain.

   Toshi has _____¢.

Solve. Choose a strategy.

- Draw a picture.
- Use models to act it out.

3. Kyle has 5 dimes. He saves another 23¢. He wants to buy a notebook that costs 80¢. How much more does he need?

   Draw or write to explain.

   _____¢

Name ______________________ Date ______________

Mental Math: Add Tens

Find each sum. Write the addition sentence.

1. 3 tens + 4 tens = 7 tens
   30 + 40 = 70

2. 4 tens + 4 tens = _____ tens
   _____ + _____ = _____

3. 2 tens + 3 tens = _____ tens
   _____ + _____ = _____

4. 3 tens + 5 tens = _____ tens
   _____ + _____ = _____

5. 7 tens + 2 tens = _____ tens
   _____ + _____ = _____

6. 1 ten + 4 tens = _____ tens
   _____ + _____ = _____

7. 4 tens + 2 tens = _____ tens
   _____ + _____ = _____

8. 3 tens + 3 tens = _____ tens
   _____ + _____ = _____

9. 7 tens + 1 ten = _____ tens
   _____ + _____ = _____

10. 2 tens + 6 tens = _____ tens
    _____ + _____ = _____

Problem Solving • Reasoning

11. Sara tossed three counters on a mat. Her total score is 90. Mark an X where the counters may have landed.

Name ______________________ Date ____________

Add Without Regrouping

Add. Use the hundred chart.

1. 19 + 20 = 39
2. 10 + 35 = ____
3. 44 + 40 = ____
4. 56 + 30 = ____
5. 14 + 80 = ____
6. 22 + 50 = ____

1	2	3	4	5	6	7	8	9	10
11	12	13	14	15	16	17	18	19	20
21	22	23	24	25	26	27	28	29	30
31	32	33	34	35	36	37	38	39	40
41	42	43	44	45	46	47	48	49	50
51	52	53	54	55	56	57	58	59	60
61	62	63	64	65	66	67	68	69	70
71	72	73	74	75	76	77	78	79	80
81	82	83	84	85	86	87	88	89	90
91	92	93	94	95	96	97	98	99	100

7. 31 + 34 = ____
8. 20 + 17 = ____
9. 40 + 33 = ____
10. 30 + 27 = ____
11. 50 + 13 = ____
12. 21 + 70 = ____
13. 10 + 13 = ____
14. 46 + 11 = ____
15. 25 + 40 = ____
16. 50 + 27 = ____

Problem Solving • Reasoning

Use the table. Solve.

Toys	Sold
T-Rexes	30
Rhino-Rexes	48

17. What is the total number of toy dinosaurs sold? ____ sold

Draw or write to explain.

Name ________________________ Date ____________

Regroup Ones

Use a workmat with [ten rod] and [unit cube].
Regroup 10 ones as 1 ten.

1. Regroup

3 tens 14 ones = 44

3 tens 14 ones → 4 tens 4 ones = 44

2. 2 tens 18 ones = ____

3. 8 tens 19 ones = ____

4. 5 tens 19 ones = ____

5. 2 tens 17 ones = ____

6. 1 ten 11 ones = ____

7. 4 tens 15 ones = ____

Problem Solving • Reasoning

8. Circle the pictures that show 59.

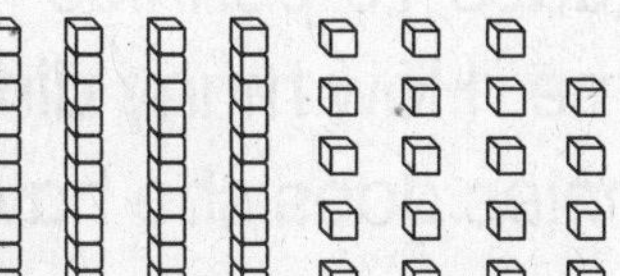

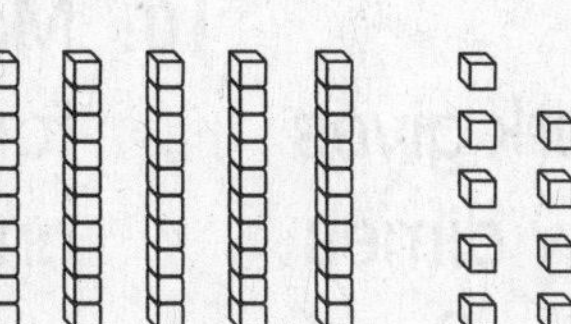

Name ____________________ Date ____________

Decide When to Regroup

Add. Indicate if you want to regroup.

	Show this many.	Add.	Do you need to regroup?	How many in all?
1.	3 tens 8 ones	4 ones	(yes) no	4 tens 2 ones
2.	5 tens 9 ones	3 ones	yes no	____ tens ____ ones
3.	2 tens 4 ones	4 ones	yes no	____ tens ____ ones
4.	1 ten 6 ones	6 ones	yes no	____ tens ____ ones
5.	4 tens 2 ones	8 ones	yes no	____ tens ____ ones
6.	7 tens 7 ones	7 ones	yes no	____ tens ____ ones
7.	4 tens 8 ones	1 one	yes no	____ tens ____ ones
8.	6 tens 4 ones	2 ones	yes no	____ tens ____ ones

Problem Solving • Reasoning

9. Maria has 4 dimes and 4 pennies. Her friend Mark gives her 9 pennies. How many dimes and pennies does she have?

____ dimes ____ pennies

10. Maria trades 10 pennies for 1 dime. How many dimes and pennies does she have now?

____ dimes ____ pennies

Name ______________________ Date ____________

Add One-Digit Numbers

Add. Regroup if you need to.

1.

	Tens	Ones
	1	
	4	3
+		8
	5	1

Workmat

Tens | Ones

2.

	Tens	Ones
	☐	
	6	2
+		8

3.

	Tens	Ones
	☐	
	4	1
+		9

4.

	Tens	Ones
	☐	
	5	9
+		3

5.

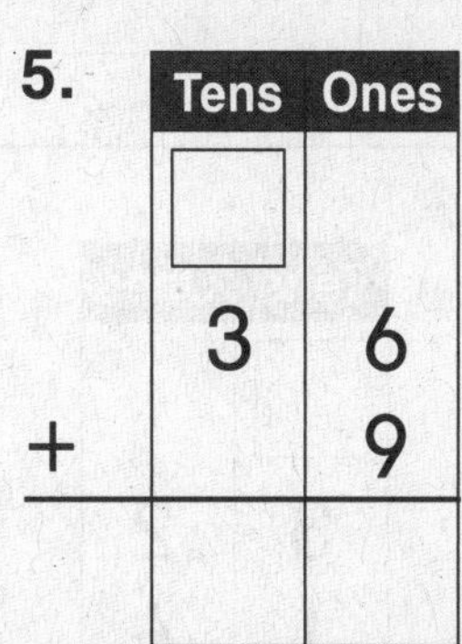

	Tens	Ones
	☐	
	3	6
+		9

6.

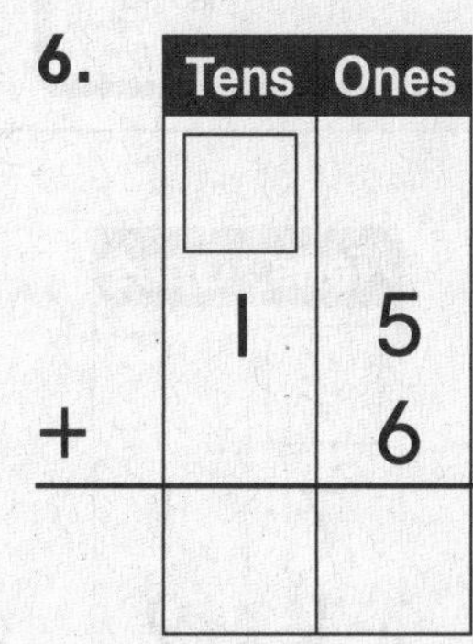

	Tens	Ones
	☐	
	1	5
+		6

7.

	Tens	Ones
	☐	
	2	2
+		7

Problem Solving • Reasoning

8. Use these numbers. 2 4 7
Write two addition problems.
Write each sum.

Add with regrouping.

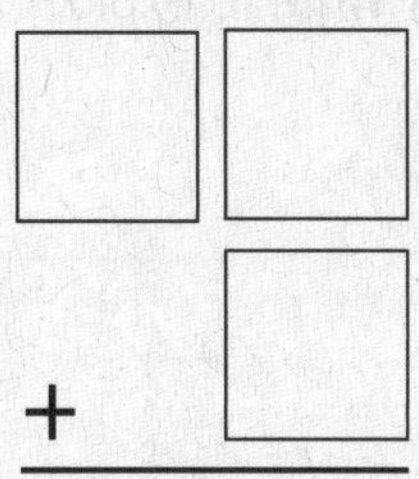

Add without regrouping.

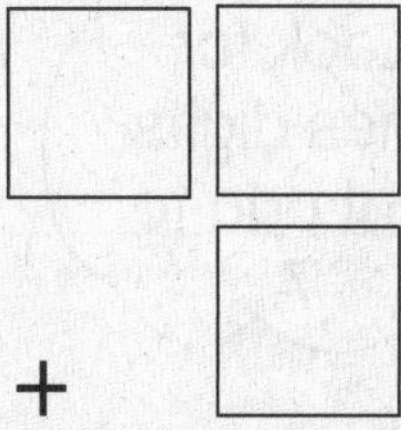

Draw or write to explain.

Name ______________________ Date ______________

Add Two-Digit Numbers

Add. Regroup if you need to. If you have ten or more ones, you need to regroup.

1.

	Tens	Ones
	1	
	2	7
+	1	8
	4	5

Workmat

Tens	Ones

2.

	Tens	Ones
	☐	
	4	6
+		9

3.

	Tens	Ones
	☐	
	6	8
+	2	2

4.

	Tens	Ones
	☐	
	1	7
+	3	8

5.

	Tens	Ones
	☐	
	7	1
+	1	9

6.

	Tens	Ones
	☐	
	3	2
+	1	6

7.

	Tens	Ones
	☐	
	5	7
+	1	3

Problem Solving • Reasoning

8. Use two numbers from below. Write a number sentence with a sum of 27.

15 11 12 19

_____ + _____ = 27

Think: Look for ones digits that add to 7.

Draw or write to explain.

Name ______________________ Date ____________

Practice Regrouping 10 to 12

Add. Regroup if you need to.

1.		2.		3.		4.	
1							
3	6	4	9	5	2	3	2
+ 4	4	+ 1	2	+	9	+ 1	0
8	0						

5.		6.		7.		8.	
7	2	6	5	4	3	1	6
+	8	+ 2	7	+ 2	8	+ 5	4

9.		10.		11.		12.	
2	6	1	6	6	2	1	5
+ 4	6	+ 1	5	+ 1	8	+ 5	7

Problem Solving • Reasoning

Use the graph. Solve each problem.

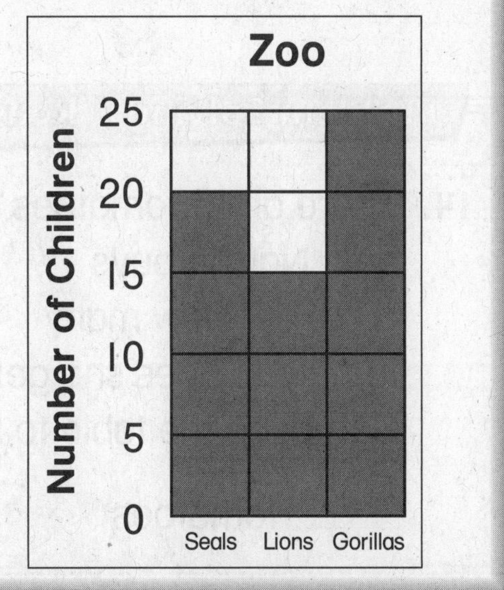

13. How many children visited the gorillas?

_____ children

14. How many children in all visited the seals and lions?

_____ children in all

Name ______________________ Date ____________

Practice Regrouping 13 to 15

Add. Regroup if you need to.

1.
	1	
	4	7
+	3	8
	8	5

2.
	2	9
+	1	4

3.
	2	6
+		8

4.
	5	5
+	1	8

5.
	1	8
+	1	6

6.
	3	6
+	2	9

7.
	7	6
+		8

8.
	3	9
+		4

9. 65 + 9

10. 27 + 7

11. 41 + 19

12. 64 + 27

13. 16 + 39

Problem Solving • Reasoning

14. There are 5 tomatoes in a box. Natalia buys 5 boxes. How many tomatoes does she get? Complete the table to help you.

Boxes	1	2	3	4	5
Tomatoes	5	10			

_____ tomatoes

Name ______________________ Date ____________

Practice Regrouping 16 to 18

Add. Regroup if you need to.

1. 28 + 68
96

2. 28 + 49

3. 62 + 17

4. 49 + 48

5. 5 + 69

6. 27 + 39

7. 13 + 44

8. 39 + 57

9. 48 + 4

10. 39 + 19

11. 46 + 2

12. 16 + 18

13. 35 + 37

14. 29 + 67

15. 38 + 47

16. 58 + 25

Problem Solving • Reasoning

17. Carol has 28 shells. She goes to the beach and collects 19 more. How many does she have in all?

_____ shells in all

Draw or write to explain.

Name ______________________ Date __________

Estimate Sums

Use the number line. Round each number to the nearest ten. Estimate the sum.

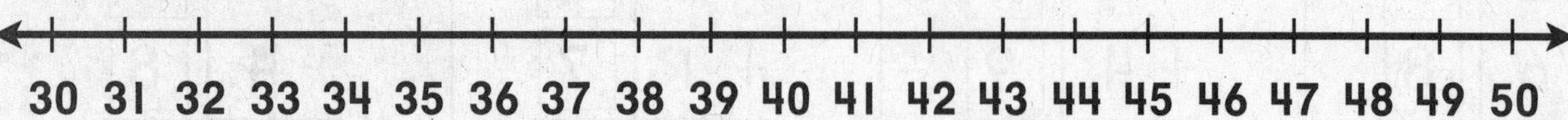

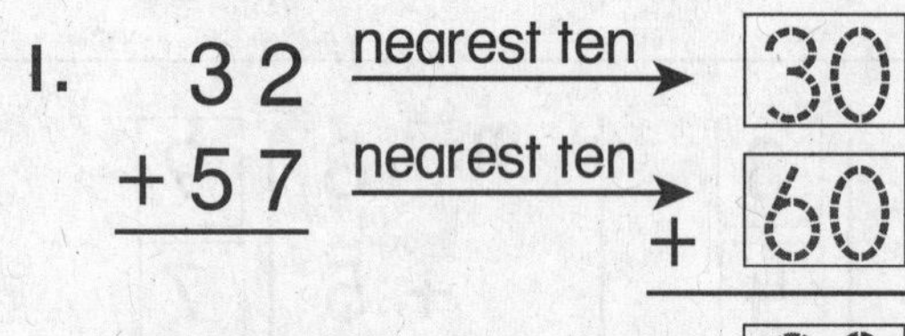

32 + 57 is about 90

2. 26 → ☐
+29 → + ☐

26 + 29 is about ☐

3. 41 → ☐
+34 → + ☐

41 + 34 is about ☐

4. 46 → ☐
+36 → + ☐

46 + 36 is about ☐

5. 22 → ☐
+39 → + ☐

22 + 39 is about ☐

6. 52 → ☐
+19 → + ☐

52 + 19 is about ☐

Problem Solving • Reasoning

7. **Estimate** The planetarium shop has 24 posters of the Milky Way and 48 posters of the Sun. About how many posters do they have?

about ______ posters

Draw or write to explain.

Name ______________________ Date __________

Problem Solving: Guess and Check

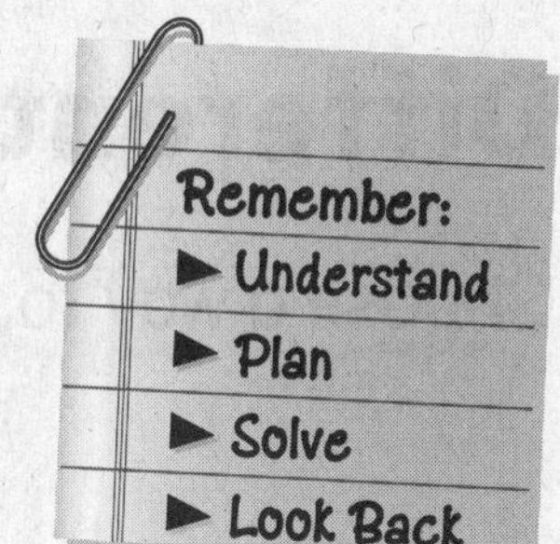

You can guess and check to solve to a problem.

Prizes	Numbers
Key chains	12
Whistles	19
Puzzles	27
Toy cars	23

Guess and check to solve each problem. Use the table.

1. Wally needs 39 prizes for the fair. Which two kinds should he buy?

   ______________ and ______________

   Think: Which two numbers have a sum of 39?

   Draw or write to explain.

2. Nora buys 42 prizes for a party. Which two kinds does she buy?

   __________ and __________

   Think: What two numbers will you choose?

   Draw or write to explain.

Solve. Choose a strategy.

- Use models to act it out.
- Draw a picture.
- Guess and check.

3. Bert's team won 4 key chains, 3 puzzles, and all of the toy cars. How many prizes did they win?

   _____ prizes

   Draw or write to explain.

Name ______________________ Date ____________

Different Ways to Add

Choose a way to solve each problem. Then add.

Ways to Add
- mental math
- hundred chart
- tens and ones blocks
- paper and pencil

1. 41 + 19 = 60	2. 39 + 20	3. 81 + 9	4. 76 + 21	5. 38 + 16
6. 28 + 66	7. 91 + 2	8. 53 + 33	9. 47 + 39	10. 51 + 41
11. 26 + 26	12. 47 + 24	13. 61 + 11	14. 80 + 19	15. 12 + 36

Problem Solving • Reasoning

16. Draw the missing tens and ones.
Complete the number sentence.

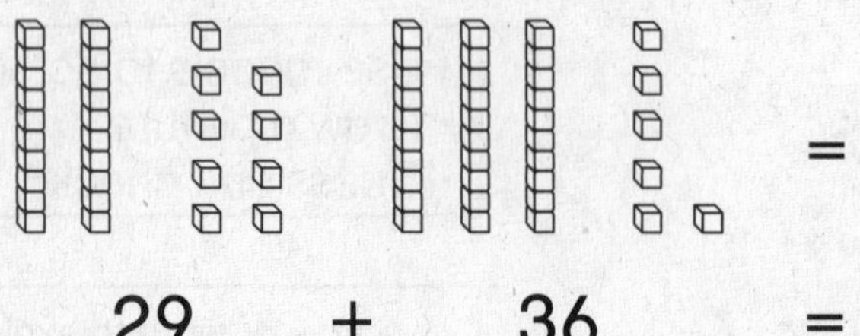
=
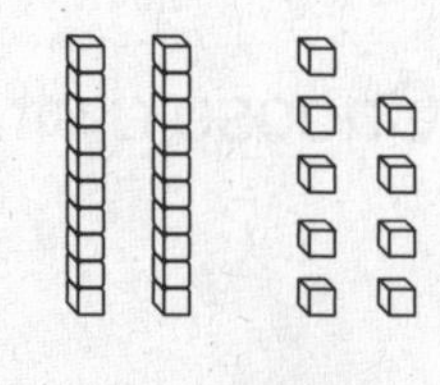

29 + 36 = ____ + 29

17. **Write About It** Explain how you found your answer.

Name ______________________ Date ____________

Horizontal Addition

Rewrite the numbers. Then add.

1. 49 + 26

   4 9
   + 2 6
   7 5

2. 53 + 39

3. 21 + 11

4. 43 + 17

5. 19 + 53

6. 27 + 32

7. 47 + 28

8. 43 + 20

9. 73 + 17

10. 62 + 36

11. 59 + 22

12. 24 + 42

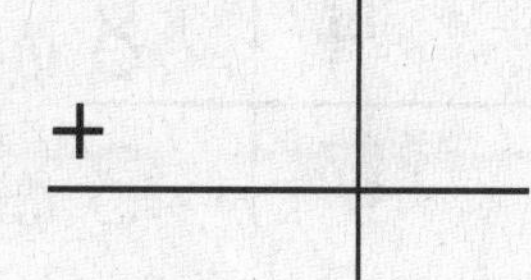

Problem Solving • Reasoning

Write a vocabulary word for each exercise.

regroup sum round

13.

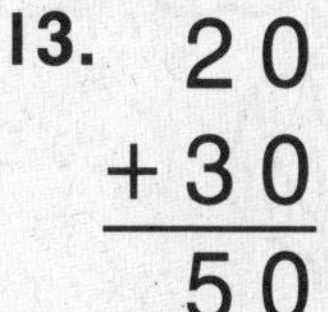

____

14.

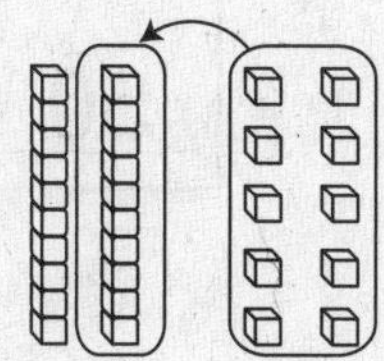

____

15. 22 nearest ten → 20

____

Name ______________________ Date ____________

Add Money

Add.

1.	2.	3.	4.	5.
58¢ + 32¢ = 90¢	52¢ + 29¢	17¢ + 25¢	59¢ + 19¢	28¢ + 8¢

6.	7.	8.	9.	10.
51¢ + 12¢	35¢ + 47¢	15¢ + 18¢	75¢ + 15¢	26¢ + 64¢

Rewrite the numbers. Then add.

11. 25¢ + 48¢ 12. 17¢ + 34¢ 13. 55¢ + 27¢ 14. 39¢ + 25¢

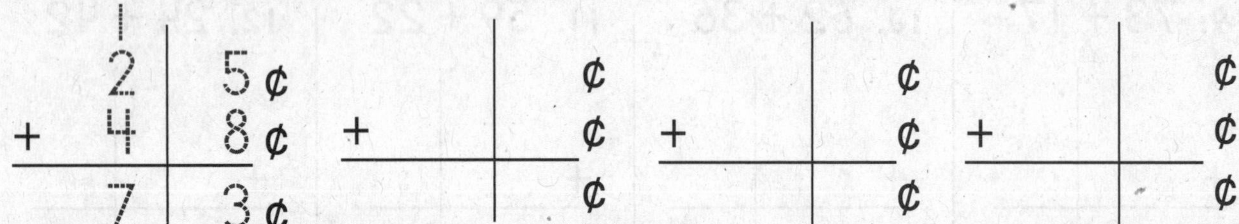

Problem Solving • Reasoning

Write About It

15. Juanita has 85¢. She wants to buy [apple] and [watermelon]. Does she have enough?

_____

Explain how you know.

____

Name ______________________ Date ______________

Algebra Readiness: Add Three Numbers

Add.

1.	2.	3.	4.	5.
16 9 +22	22 18 +20	26 19 + 3	25 22 +21	29 31 +27

6.	7.	8.	9.	10.
12 40 + 7	60 17 + 5	25 25 +25	31 21 +11	1 39 +20

11.	12.	13.	14.	15.
11 12 +13	29 25 +21	10 12 +19	29 40 +11	19 61 +15

Problem Solving • Reasoning

Complete the number sentences.

Think: Work inside the ( ) first.

16. (13 + 2) + 10 = ? ____   13 + (2 + 10) = ? ____

____ + 10 = ____   13 + ____ = ____

17. (18 + 1) + 11 = ? ____   18 + (1 + 11) = ? ____

____ + 11 = ____   18 + ____ = ____

Name ______________________ Date ____________

Problem Solving: Use Data From a Picture

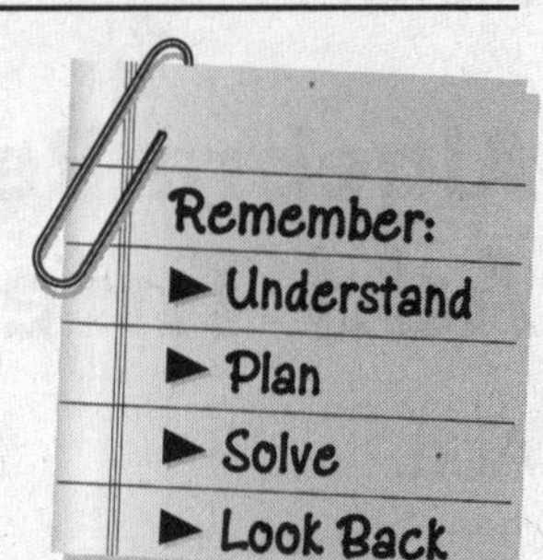

You can use data from a picture to solve a problem.

35¢
crayons

50¢
coloring book

20¢
stickers

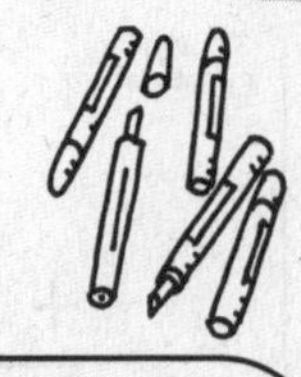
40¢
markers

Use the pictures to solve each problem.

1. Kayla buys a set of stickers and a coloring book. How much does she spend?

   ____

   Think: What information do I need from the picture?

   Draw or write to explain.

---

2. Jeremy wants to buy a coloring book and markers. What is the total cost?

   ____

   Think: How much does each item cost?

   Draw or write to explain.

Solve. Choose a strategy.

- Write a number sentence.
- Use models to act it out.
- Guess and check.

3. The store has 12 toy zebras. 8 of them are sold. How many toy zebras are left?

   ____ zebras are left

   Think: Do I add or subtract?

   Draw or write to explain.

Name ______________________ Date ____________

Mental Math: Subtract Tens

Find each difference. Write the subtraction sentence.

1. 6 tens – 3 tens = 3 tens
   60 – 30 = 30

2. 4 tens – 3 tens = ____ ten
   ____ – ____ = ____

3. 9 tens – 4 tens = ____ tens
   ____ – ____ = ____

4. 6 tens – 2 tens = ____ tens
   ____ – ____ = ____

5. 5 tens – 3 tens = ____ tens
   ____ – ____ = ____

6. 8 tens – 6 tens = ____ tens
   ____ – ____ = ____

7. 9 tens – 1 ten = ____ tens
   ____ – ____ = ____

8. 5 tens – 5 tens = ____ tens
   ____ – ____ = ____

Problem Solving • Reasoning

Read the clues. Write each number.

9. You say it when you count by tens. It is greater than 0. It is less than 20. ____

Draw or write to explain.

10. You say it when you count by tens. It is less than 60. It is greater than 40. ____

Draw or write to explain.

Name ______________________ Date ____________

Subtract Without Regrouping

Subtract.
Use the hundred chart.

1	2	3	4	5	6	7	8	9	10
11	12	13	14	15	16	17	18	19	20
21	22	23	24	25	26	27	28	29	30
31	32	33	34	35	36	37	38	39	40
41	42	43	44	45	46	47	48	49	50
51	52	53	54	55	56	57	58	59	60
61	62	63	64	65	66	67	68	69	70
71	72	73	74	75	76	77	78	79	80
81	82	83	84	85	86	87	88	89	90
91	92	93	94	95	96	97	98	99	100

1. 51 − 20 = 31
2. 99 − 40 = ______
3. 67 − 60 = ______
4. 44 − 30 = ______
5. 39 − 10 = ______
6. 85 − 50 = ______

7. $\begin{array}{r} 55 \\ -30 \\ \hline \end{array}$

8. $\begin{array}{r} 77 \\ -40 \\ \hline \end{array}$

9. $\begin{array}{r} 86 \\ -54 \\ \hline \end{array}$

10. $\begin{array}{r} 27 \\ -20 \\ \hline \end{array}$

11. $\begin{array}{r} 99 \\ -60 \\ \hline \end{array}$

12. $\begin{array}{r} 53 \\ -31 \\ \hline \end{array}$

13. $\begin{array}{r} 73 \\ -40 \\ \hline \end{array}$

14. $\begin{array}{r} 87 \\ -60 \\ \hline \end{array}$

15. $\begin{array}{r} 77 \\ -50 \\ \hline \end{array}$

16. $\begin{array}{r} 38 \\ -10 \\ \hline \end{array}$

Problem Solving • Reasoning

17. Thirty-three fish are in a pet store aquarium. Ten are sold. How many fish are left in the aquarium?

______ fish

Draw or write to explain.

Name ______________________ Date __________

Regroup Tens

Use Workmat 3 with [tens] and [ones] if you like.
Regroup 1 ten as 10 ones.

1. 55 → Regroup → 4 tens 15 ones

2. 39 = ____ tens ____ ones | 3. 56 = ____ tens ____ ones

4. 73 = ____ tens ____ ones | 5. 27 = ____ tens ____ ones

6. 51 = ____ tens ____ ones | 7. 85 = ____ tens ____ ones

8. 48 = ____ tens ____ ones | 9. 93 = ____ tens ____ ones

10. 53 = ____ tens ____ ones | 11. 36 = ____ tens ____ ones

12. 77 = ____ tens ____ ones | 13. 24 = ____ tens ____ ones

Problem Solving • Reasoning

Write About It

14. Fred showed 29 this way. Tori showed 29 this way.

Both are correct. Explain why.

Name ______________________ Date __________

Decide When to Regroup

Use Workmat 3 with [tens] and [ones] if you like, to complete the chart.

	Show this many.	Take away.	Do you need to regroup?	How many are left?
1.	4 tens 8 ones	9 ones	(yes) no	3 tens 9 ones
2.	7 tens 3 ones	6 ones	yes no	___ tens ___ ones
3.	6 tens 2 ones	8 ones	yes no	___ tens ___ ones
4.	9 tens 1 one	1 one	yes no	___ tens ___ ones
5.	3 tens 2 ones	3 ones	yes no	___ tens ___ ones
6.	7 tens 9 ones	5 ones	yes no	___ tens ___ ones
7.	1 ten 6 ones	7 ones	yes no	___ tens ___ ones
8.	5 tens 2 ones	5 ones	yes no	___ tens ___ ones

Problem Solving • Reasoning

9. Johnny has 3 dimes and 2 pennies. He wants to give Sid 9 pennies. Explain how he can do this.

10. Johnny gave Sid the 9 pennies. Find out how much money Johnny has left.

_____¢

Draw or write to explain.

Name ______________________ Date ____________

Subtract One-Digit Numbers

Use Workmat 3 with [tens block] and [ones block] if you like.
Subtract. Regroup if you need to.

1.

Tens	Ones
3	13
~~4~~	~~3~~
−	5
3	8

2.

Tens	Ones
7	3
−	6

3.

Tens	Ones
5	0
−	9

4.

Tens	Ones
8	8
−	8

5.

Tens	Ones
3	5
−	8

6.

Tens	Ones
2	2
−	7

7.

Tens	Ones
9	4
−	6

8.

Tens	Ones
3	1
−	2

Problem Solving • Reasoning

Use [tens block] and [ones block] to solve if you like.

9. The candle shop had 64 candles. On Thursday, 9 candles were sold. How many candles were still at the candle shop?

_____ candles

Draw or write to explain.

Name ______________________ Date ____________

Subtract Two-Digit Numbers

Subtract. Regroup if you need to.

1.

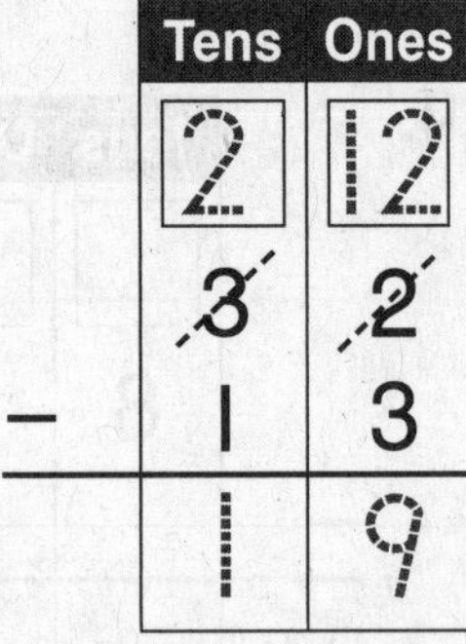

2.

	Tens	Ones
	7	7
−	2	9

3.

	Tens	Ones
	8	2
−	4	5

4.

	Tens	Ones
	9	1
−	2	5

5.

	Tens	Ones
	3	9
−	1	5

6.

	Tens	Ones
	6	7
−	2	9

7.

	Tens	Ones
	4	6
−	3	7

8.

	Tens	Ones
	5	5
−	2	1

Problem Solving • Reasoning

Use tens blocks and ones blocks to solve if you like.

9. Show 57 with your blocks. Pick a number to subtract in which you need to regroup. Write the subtraction problem and solve.

Draw or write to explain.

Name ________________ Date ________

Problem Solving: Use Models to Act It Out

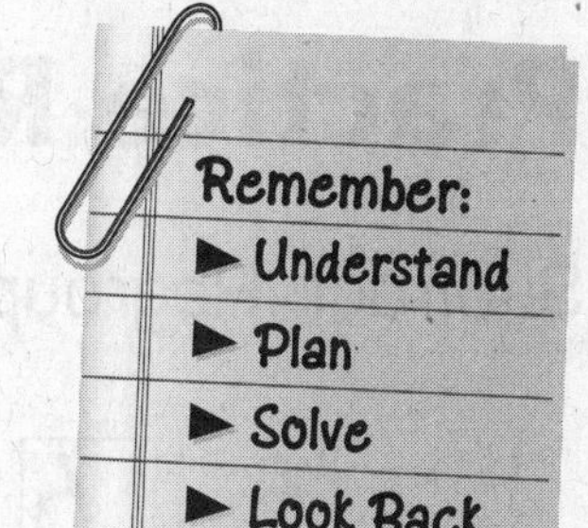

You can solve some problems by acting them out with tens and ones blocks.
Solve each problem. Use blocks if you need to.

1. Jan's team scored 15 runs. Jim's team scored 9 runs. How many runs were scored in all?

   Think: What do I need to find out?

   Draw or write to explain.

   _____ runs

2. Daniel counted 22 stars in the sky. Eva counted 14. How many more stars did Daniel count?

   Think: Do I add or subtract?

   Draw or write to explain.

   _____ stars

Solve. Choose a strategy.

- Draw a picture.
- Use models to act it out.

3. Mrs. Lee has 5 hens. If each hen lays 2 eggs, how many eggs will she have?

   Draw or write to explain.

   _____ eggs

Name ______________________ Date ____________

Practice Regrouping With 10 or 11

Subtract. Regroup if you need to.

1.

	Tens	Ones
	6	16
	~~7~~	~~6~~
−	1	8
	5	8

2.

	Tens	Ones
	8	6
−		4

3.

	Tens	Ones
	3	1
−	1	5

4.

	Tens	Ones
	8	1
−	1	1

5.

	Tens	Ones
	5	0
−	2	2

6.

	Tens	Ones
	7	1
−	3	2

7.

	Tens	Ones
	9	0
−	4	4

8.

	Tens	Ones
	2	0
−		6

9.

	Tens	Ones
	6	1
−	5	1

10.

	Tens	Ones
	4	0
−	1	3

11.

	Tens	Ones
	2	1
−	1	7

12.

	Tens	Ones
	9	1
−	6	6

Problem Solving • Reasoning

13. According to the graph, which color toothbrush was bought the most?

____

14. How many more purple toothbrushes were bought than yellow?

______

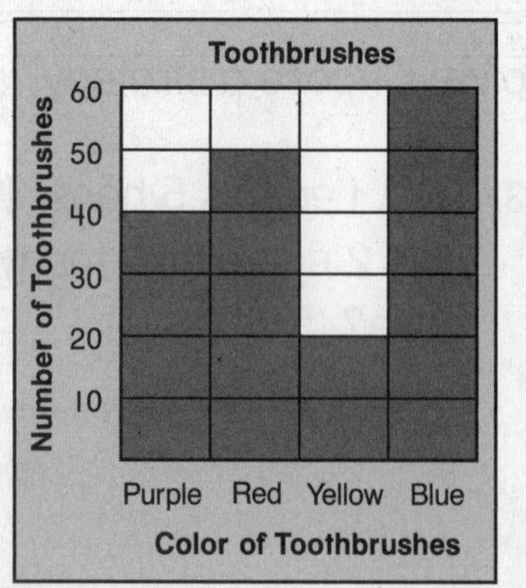

Name ______________________ Date ____________

Practice Regrouping With 12 to 14

Subtract. Regroup if you need to.

1.
Tens	Ones
1	14
2	4
− 1	7
	7

2.
Tens	Ones
5	2
−	8

3.
Tens	Ones
4	3
− 2	2

4.
Tens	Ones
7	1
− 4	3

5.
Tens	Ones
3	1
− 1	8

6.
Tens	Ones
8	1
− 3	6

7.
Tens	Ones
9	4
− 1	5

8.
Tens	Ones
6	3
− 1	0

9. $34 - 14$

10. $50 - 19$

11. $42 - 26$

12. $72 - 33$

13. $41 - 18$

Problem Solving • Reasoning

14. Some numbers on the work schedule were accidentally left out. Find the missing numbers.

CLERK	HOURS Saturday	Sunday	Total
Malika	4		12
Quinn		8	14
Lucy	8	8	16
Ricky		4	8

Name ______________________ Date ____________

Practice Regrouping With 15 to 18

Use a paper clip and pencil. Spin the spinner. Write each number in the box. Subtract. Connect the dots as you complete the problems.

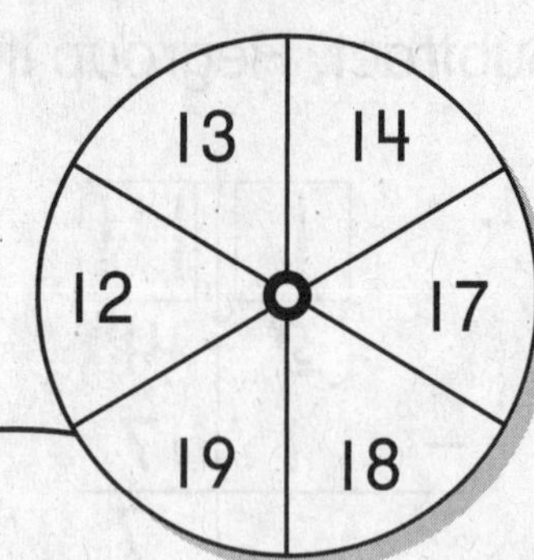

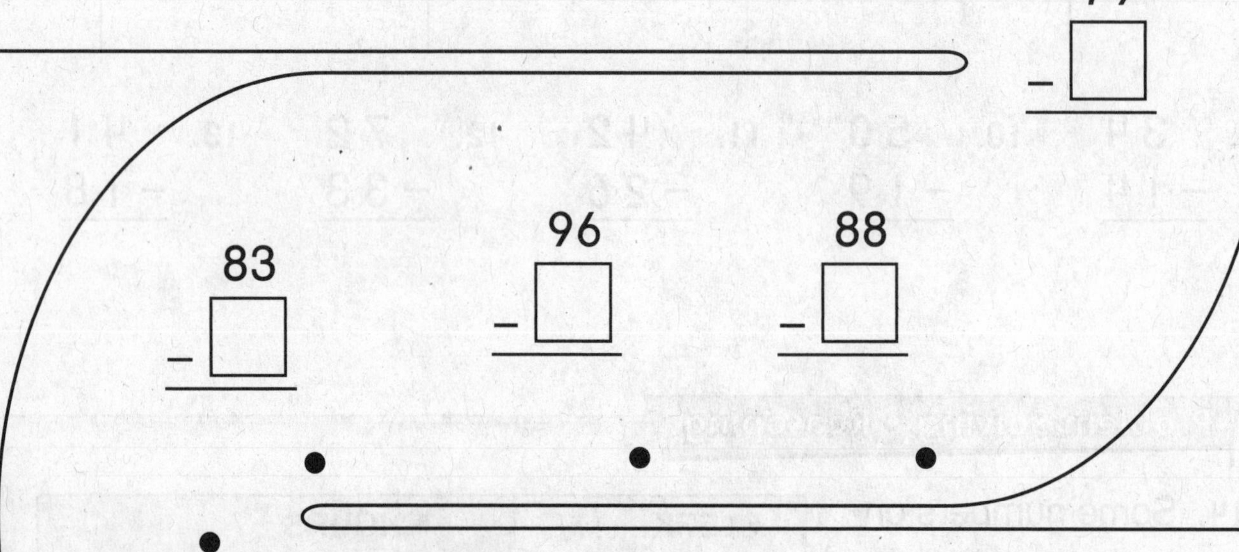

Name ______________________ Date __________

Estimate Differences

Use the number line. Round each number to the nearest ten. Estimate the difference.

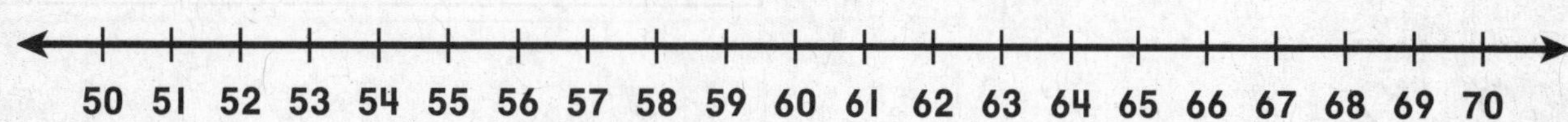

1. 66 nearest ten → 70
 − 51 nearest ten → − 50
 66 − 51 is about 20

2. 64 → ☐
 − 53 → − ☐
 64 − 53 is about ☐

3. 59 → ☐
 − 53 → − ☐
 59 − 53 is about ☐

4. 69 → ☐
 − 54 → − ☐
 69 − 54 is about ☐

5. 54 → ☐
 − 50 → − ☐
 54 − 50 is about ☐

6. 68 → ☐
 − 56 → − ☐
 68 − 56 is about ☐

Problem Solving • Reasoning

7. **Estimate** Raquel had 69 buttons. She gave Leroy 54 buttons. About how many buttons did Raquel keep?

 _____ buttons

Draw or write to explain.

Name ______________________ Date __________

Different Ways to Subtract

Choose a way to solve each problem.
Then subtract.

Ways to Subtract
- paper and pencil
- tens and ones blocks
- hundred chart
- mental math

1. 2 12 ~~3~~ ~~2~~ − 15 17	2. 82 − 36	3. 71 − 46	4. 49 − 31	5. 93 − 9
6. 66 − 52	7. 29 − 19	8. 30 − 15	9. 99 − 88	10. 85 − 29
11. 59 − 36	12. 91 − 56	13. 83 − 33	14. 71 − 45	15. 44 − 20

Problem Solving • Reasoning

Patterns

Find each difference.
Look for a pattern.
Write the next exercise in the box.

66	55	44	33	☐
− 11	− 11	− 11	− 11	− ☐
				☐

Name ______________________ Date ____________

Horizontal Subtraction

Rewrite the numbers. Then subtract.

1. 73 − 24

	6	13
	7	3
−	2	4
	4	9

2. 62 − 45

3. 89 − 54

4. 34 − 6

5. 12 − 11

6. 88 − 69

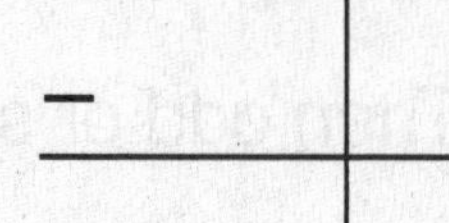

7. 59 − 41

8. 72 − 33

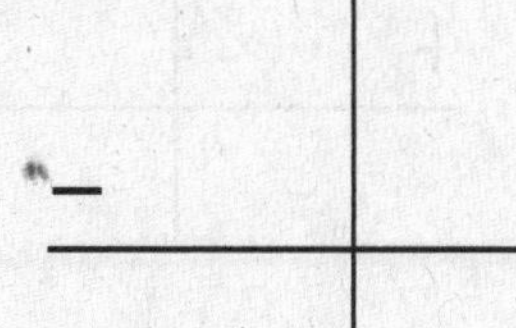

9. 96 − 61

10. 86 − 47

11. 21 − 7

12. 91 − 59

Problem Solving • Reasoning

13. Lola has 62 stamps in her collection. Anita has 15 stamps fewer than Lola. How many stamps does Anita have?

_____ stamps

14. **Write Your Own** Write an addition story problem about another kind of collection. Then solve.

Draw or write to explain.

Name ______________________ Date ____________

Add and Subtract Money

Add or subtract.

1.	2.	3.	4.	5.
$\begin{array}{r} {}^{5\ 15} \\ \not{6}\not{5}¢ \\ -\ 17¢ \\ \hline 48¢ \end{array}$	$\begin{array}{r} 51¢ \\ +\ 39¢ \\ \hline \end{array}$	$\begin{array}{r} 29¢ \\ -\ 12¢ \\ \hline \end{array}$	$\begin{array}{r} 73¢ \\ -\ 57¢ \\ \hline \end{array}$	$\begin{array}{r} 82¢ \\ +\ 17¢ \\ \hline \end{array}$

6.	7.	8.	9.	10.
$\begin{array}{r} 41¢ \\ -\ 36¢ \\ \hline \end{array}$	$\begin{array}{r} 50¢ \\ +\ 46¢ \\ \hline \end{array}$	$\begin{array}{r} 39¢ \\ +\ 39¢ \\ \hline \end{array}$	$\begin{array}{r} 82¢ \\ -\ 49¢ \\ \hline \end{array}$	$\begin{array}{r} 32¢ \\ +\ 26¢ \\ \hline \end{array}$

Rewrite the numbers. Then add or subtract.

11. 62¢ − 53¢

−

12. 69¢ + 17¢

13. 95¢ − 69¢

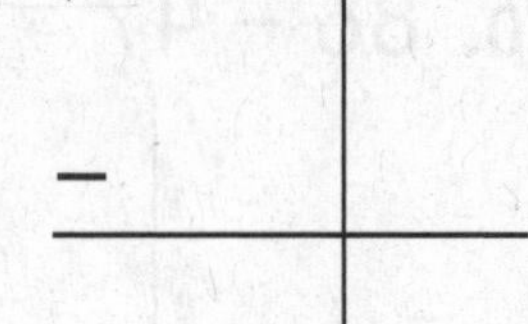

14. 35¢ + 9¢

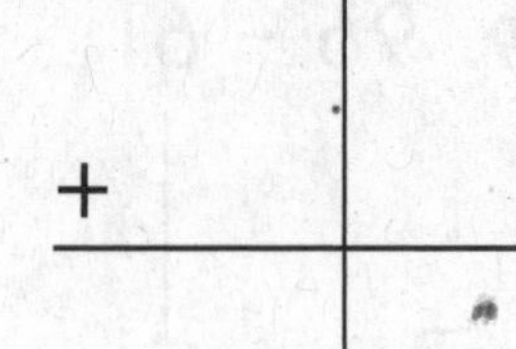

Problem Solving • Reasoning

15. How much money do you need to buy two chocolate bars? _____ ¢

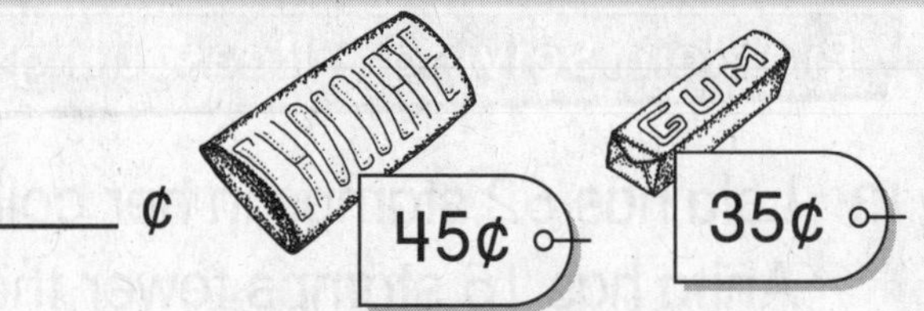

16. You have 9 dimes. You buy a chocolate bar and a pack of gum. How much money do you have left?

____

Draw or write to explain.

Name ______________________ Date __________

Algebra Readiness: Check Subtraction

Subtract. Check by adding.

1. $\begin{array}{r} 57 \\ -38 \\ \hline 19 \end{array}$ $\begin{array}{r} 19 \\ +38 \\ \hline 57 \end{array}$

2. $\begin{array}{r} 25 \\ -\ \ 6 \\ \hline \end{array}$ + ____

3. $\begin{array}{r} 26 \\ -20 \\ \hline \end{array}$ + ____

4. $\begin{array}{r} 83 \\ -61 \\ \hline \end{array}$ + ____

5. $\begin{array}{r} 93 \\ -17 \\ \hline \end{array}$ + ____

6. $\begin{array}{r} 29 \\ -19 \\ \hline \end{array}$ + ____

7. $\begin{array}{r} 53 \\ -22 \\ \hline \end{array}$ + ____

8. $\begin{array}{r} 48 \\ -36 \\ \hline \end{array}$ + ____

Problem Solving • Reasoning

9. After you regroup, you have 4 tens and 19 ones. What number did you start with?

____

10. **Write Your Own** Write a story problem about fish that has a difference of 10.

Draw or write to explain.

Name ______________________ Date ____________

Problem Solving: Use a Table

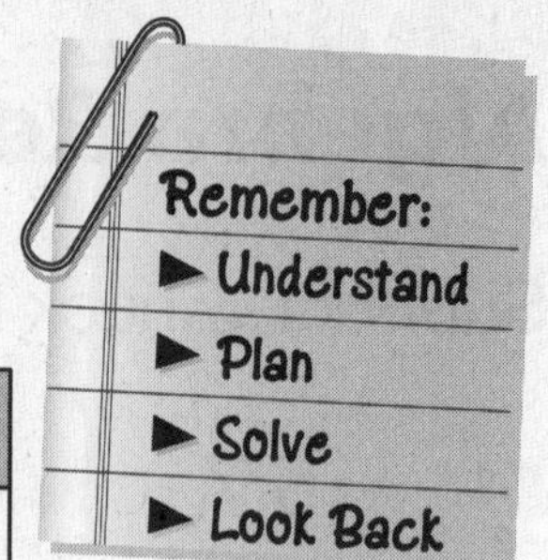

You can use the information in a table to solve a problem. The table shows the number of second graders who play each game at recess.

2nd Graders	Recess Games
35	Handball
46	Soccer
12	Hopscotch

1. How many more second graders play soccer than hopscotch?

   Think: Do I add or subtract?

   _____ second graders

   Draw or write to explain.

2. If all of the hopscotch players decide to join the handball players, how many will be playing handball?

   Think: Which numbers should I use?

   _____ players

   Draw or write to explain.

Solve. Choose a strategy.

- Use a table.
- Find a pattern.
- Write a number sentence.

3. If 18 girls are playing soccer, how many soccer players are boys?

   _____ boys

   Draw or write to explain.

 Use with text pages 287–289.

Name ______________________ Date ____________

Plane Shapes

Color the shapes that match each plane shape.

1. rectangle

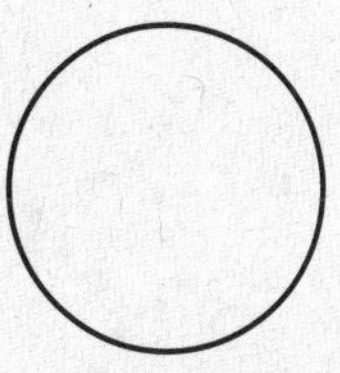
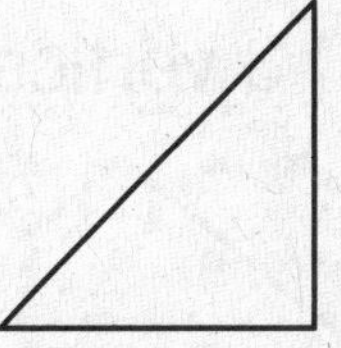

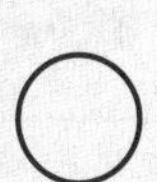

2. circle

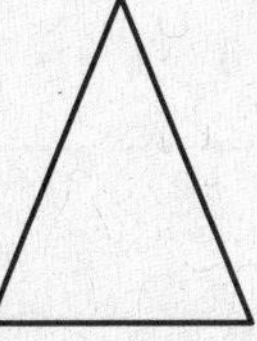

3. triangle

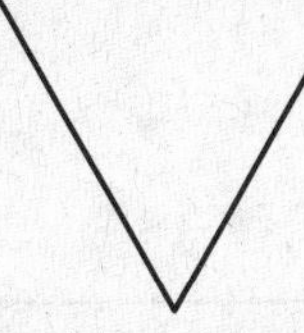
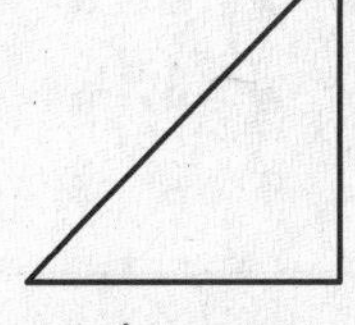

4. square

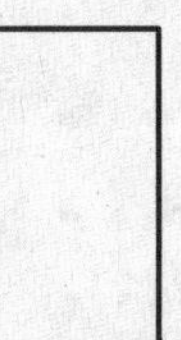

Problem Solving • Reasoning

5. Color all the shapes below that are triangles. Put an X on the shapes that are not triangles.

triangle

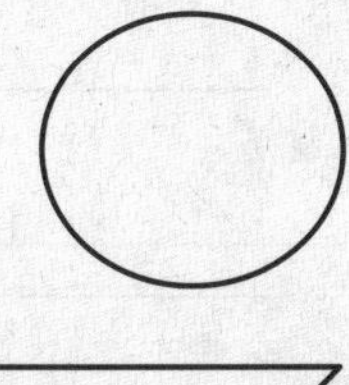
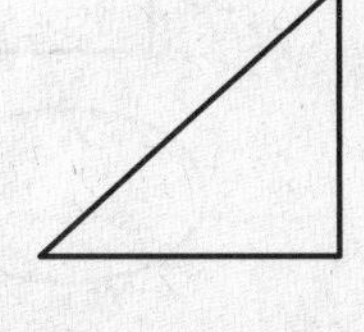

Name ______________________ Date ____________

Sides and Vertices

Draw each figure.

1. 3 sides 3 vertices

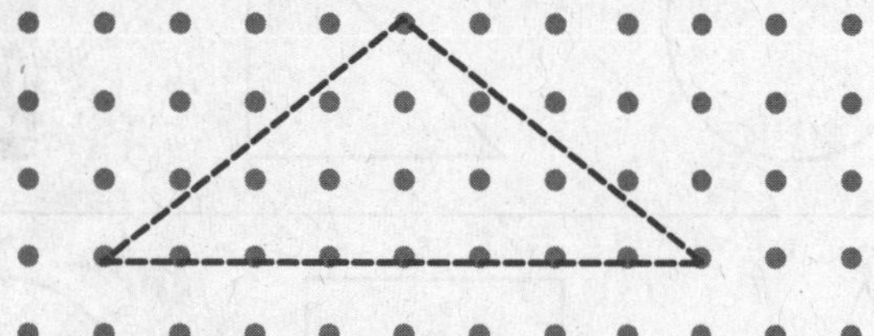

2. 5 sides 5 vertices

3. 0 sides 0 vertices

4. 4 sides 4 vertices

5. 6 sides 6 vertices

6. 4 equal sides 4 vertices

Problem Solving • Reasoning

7. Who drew each shape?

- Leyla drew a shape with 0 sides and 0 vertices.
- Scott did not draw the oval.
- Ruby drew a shape with 4 vertices.

Next to each shape, write the name of the child who drew it.

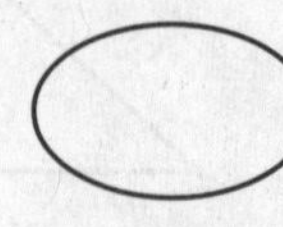 ____________

 ____________

____

Name ______________________ Date ____________

Solid Shapes

Circle the objects that match the solid shape.

1.   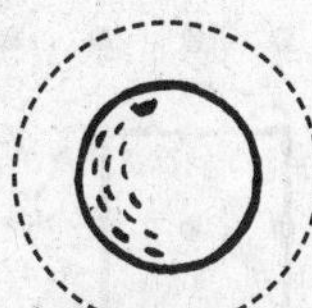 

2. 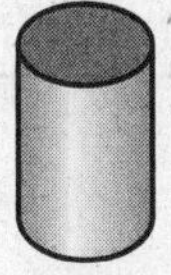 

3.  

4.    

5. 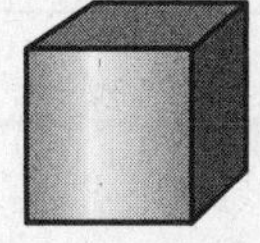   

Problem Solving • Reasoning

6. Circle the solids that roll.
Put an X on the solids that slide.

7. **Write About It** Do any solids roll and slide? Explain your answer.

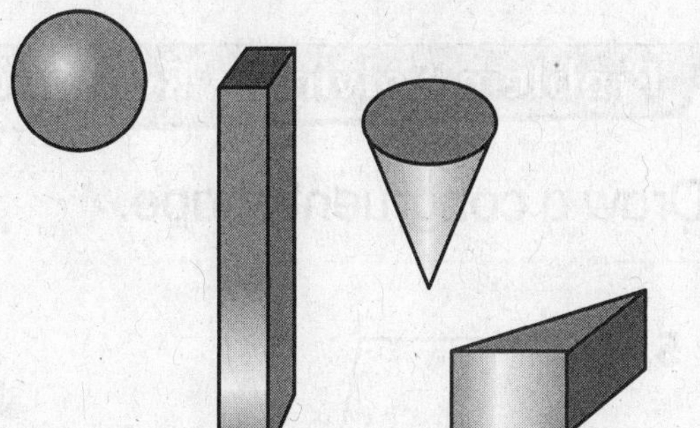

Name ________________________ Date ____________

Congruent Shapes

Circle the shape that is congruent to the first shape.

1. 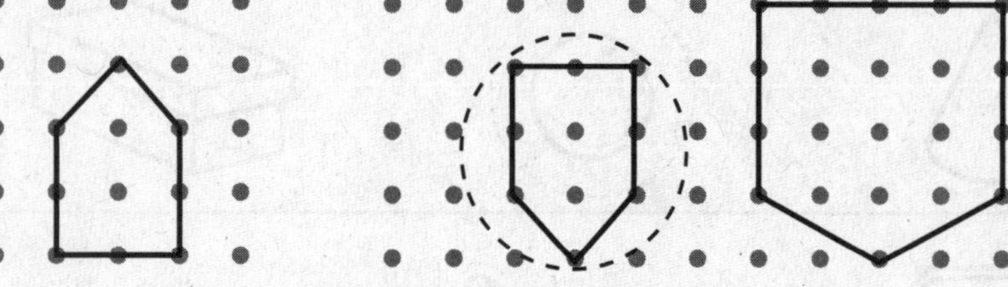

2. 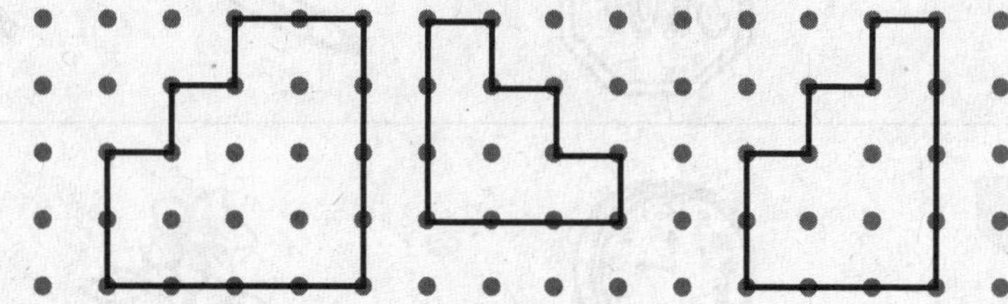

3. 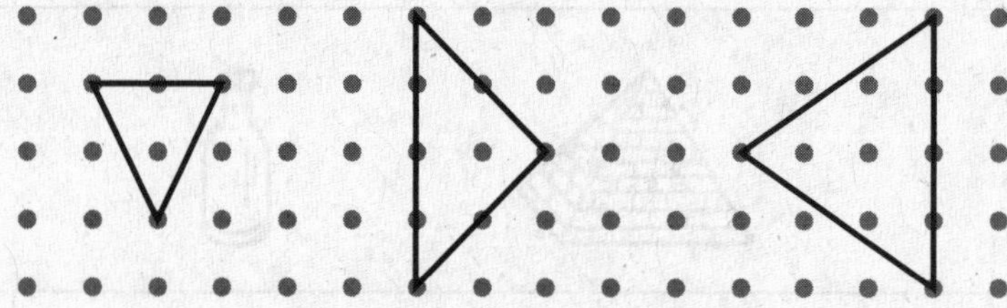

4. 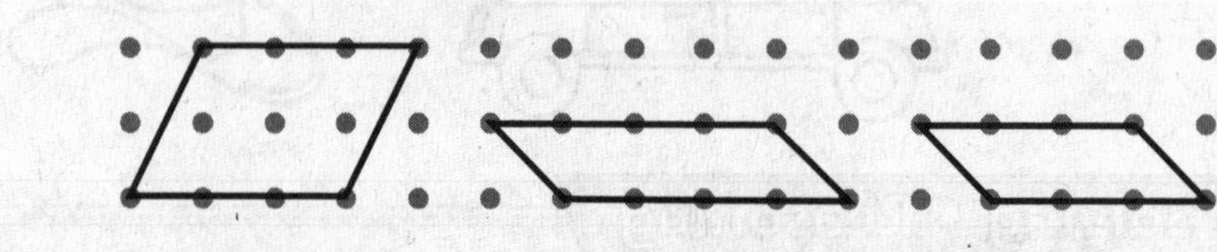

Problem Solving • Reasoning

Draw a congruent shape.

5. 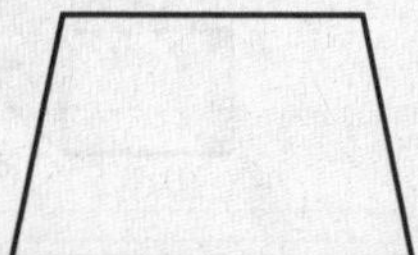

6. 

Name ______________________ Date ____________

Make New Shapes

Use the pattern blocks. Make the shape shown.
Trace around the blocks.
Make a new shape. Trace around the blocks.

1. Use these blocks.

2 

2

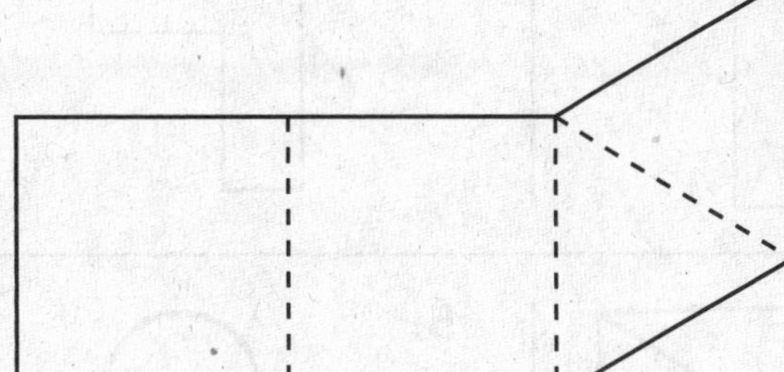

2. Use these blocks.

2 

1

Problem Solving • Reasoning

Write About It

3. Trace and cut out the shape. Use the two rectangles to make new shapes. Draw the shapes you make.

Name ______________________ Date ____________

Symmetry

Draw a line of symmetry. Cross out the shapes that do not have symmetry.

1.

2.
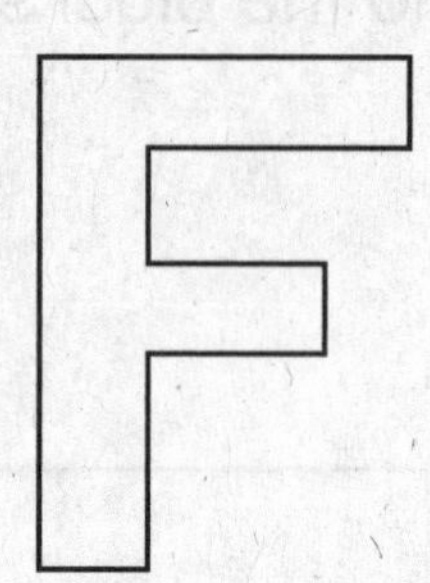

3.
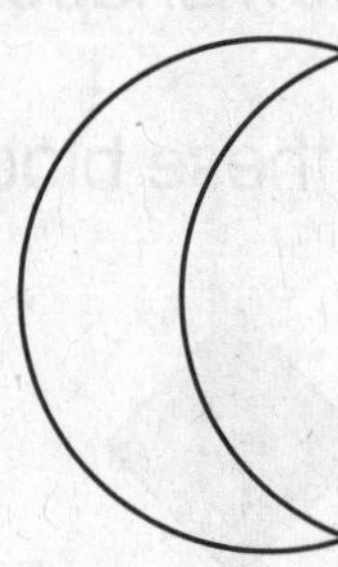

4.
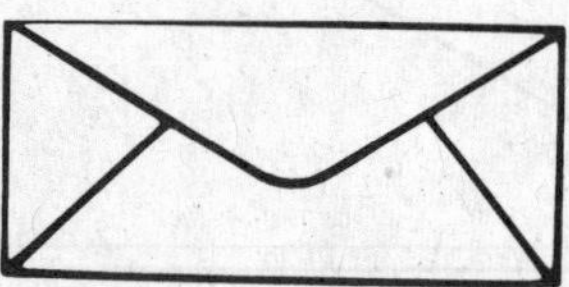

5.

6.
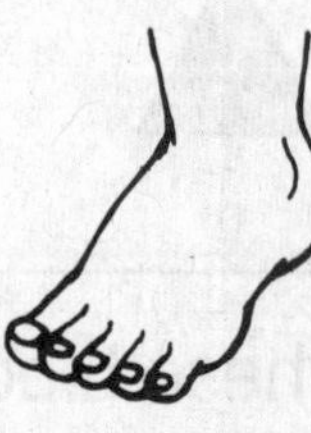

7.

8.

9.

Problem Solving • Reasoning

10. Draw two lines of symmetry.

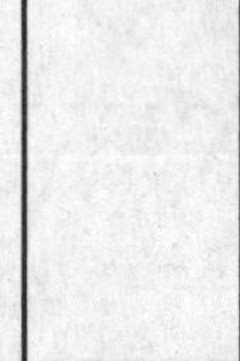

How many equal parts did you make? _____

11. Draw one line of symmetry.

How many equal parts did you make? _____

Name ______________________ Date __________

Problem Solving: Find a Pattern

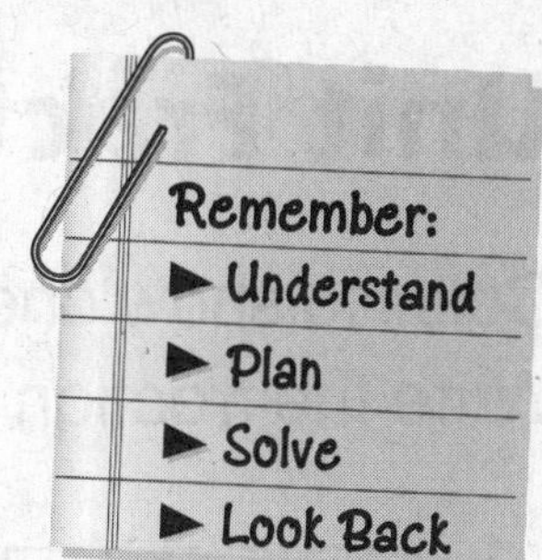

You can describe the shapes in a pattern to tell what is likely to come next.

Draw the shape that is likely to come next.

1. 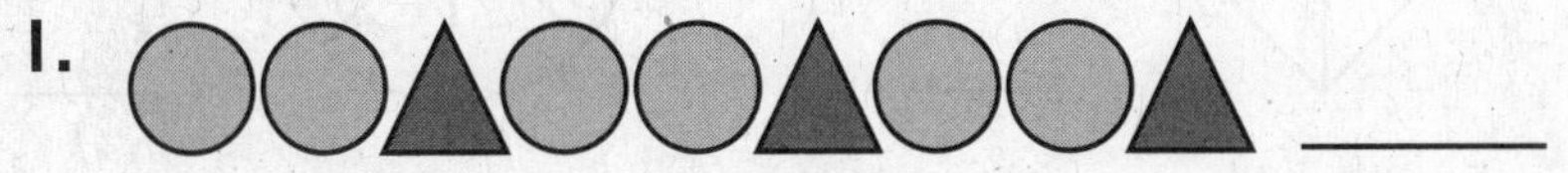 ______

Think: What shape comes after the triangle?

2. ______

Think: What is the pattern?

Solve. Choose a strategy.

- Draw a picture.
- Write a number sentence.

3. Nina has this pattern in her sticker book. Draw the next shape.

 ______

4. If star stickers cost 1 dime each, how much will Nina need to buy 5 stars?

______¢

Draw or write to explain.

Name ________________ Date ________

Unit Fractions

Color to show one shaded part.
Write the fraction for the shaded part.

1. 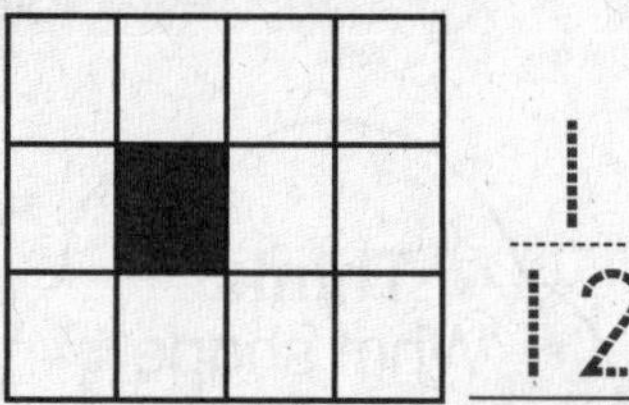

2.  ____

3.  ____

4. 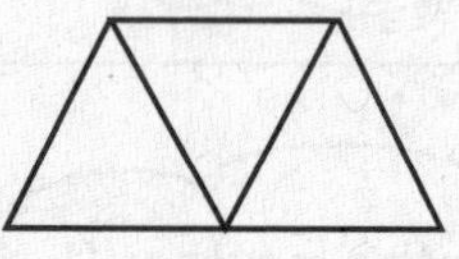 ____

5.  ____

6. 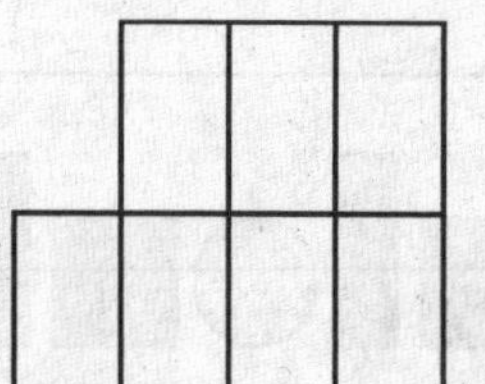 ____

7.  ____

8. 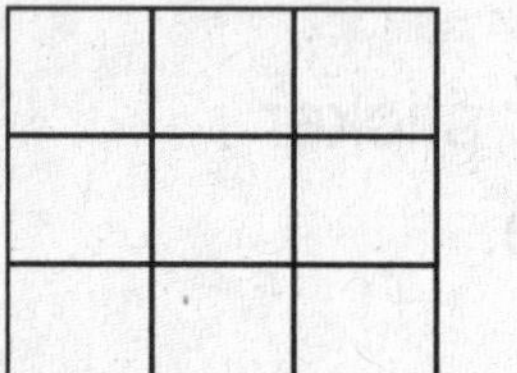 ____

9. 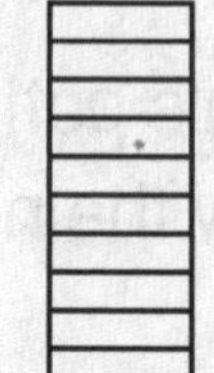 ____

Problem Solving • Reasoning

10. Look at the pattern blocks.

What fraction of the rectangle forms a triangle?

____

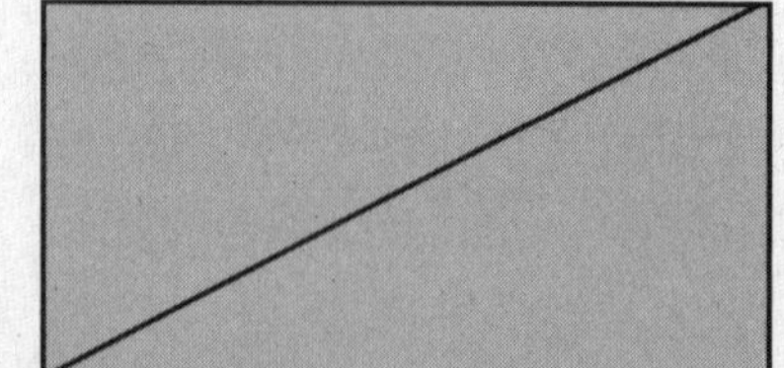

Name ______________________ Date ____________

More About Fractions

Color to show the number of shaded parts.
Write the fraction for the shaded parts.

1. 3 shaded parts

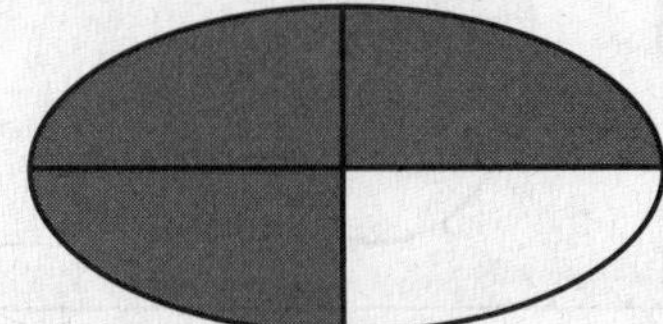

2. 3 shaded parts

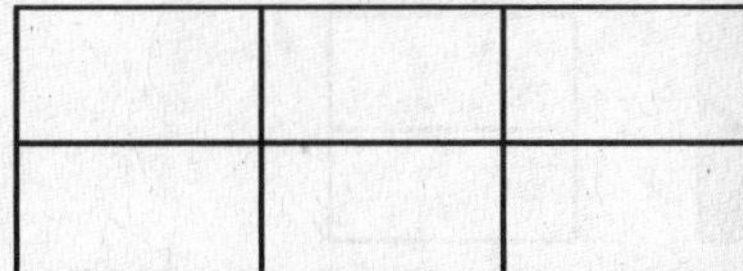

____

3. 4 shaded parts

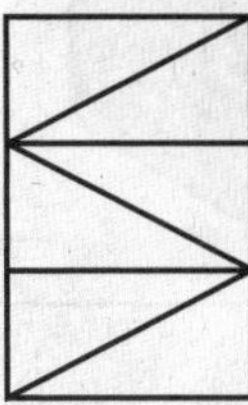

____

4. 1 shaded part

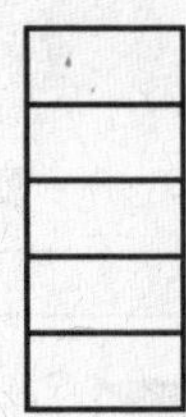

____

5. 1 shaded part

____

6. 2 shaded parts

____

Problem Solving • Reasoning

7. Count the coins. Write the amount.

Draw or write to explain.

____ ¢

Name ______________________________ Date ______________

Wholes and Parts

Write the fraction for the shaded parts.

1. 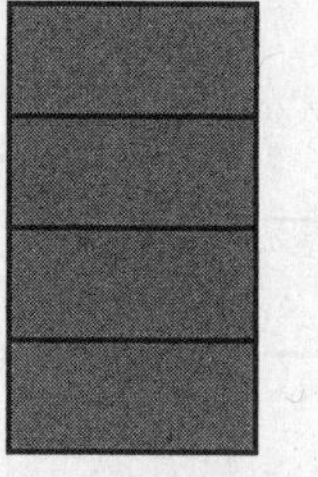  ______

2. 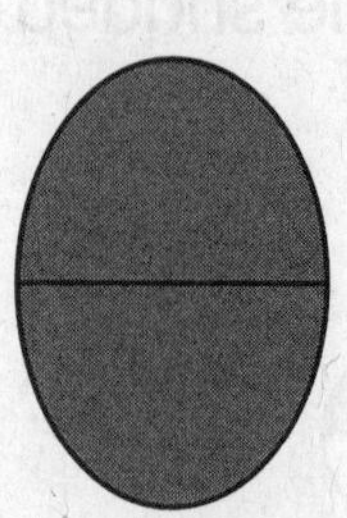 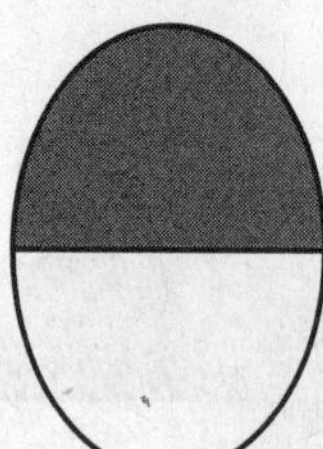 ______

3. 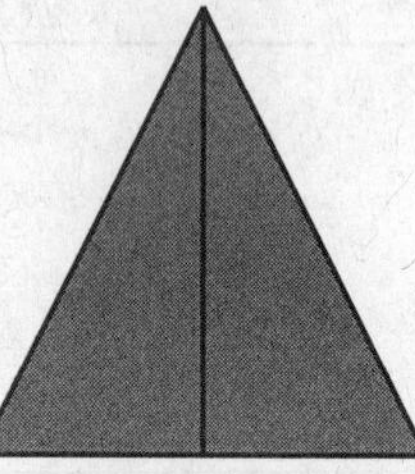 ______

4. 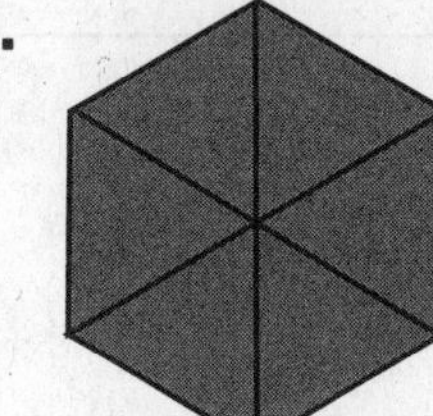 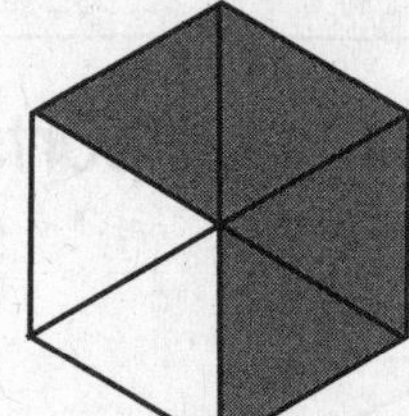 ______

5.   ______

6. 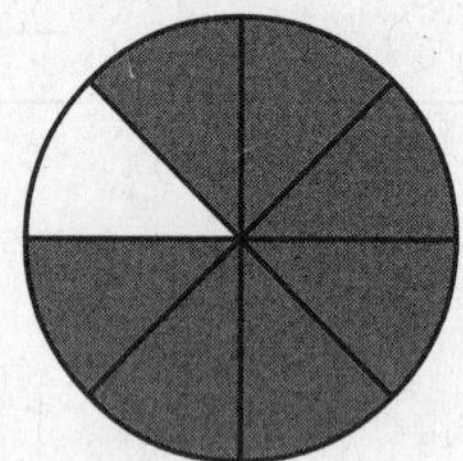 ______

Problem Solving • Reasoning

7. These fractions fell off the chart. Where do they belong? Write each fraction on the chart.

$\frac{1}{3}$ $\frac{7}{7}$ $\frac{7}{4}$ $\frac{6}{6}$ $\frac{5}{6}$ $\frac{8}{3}$

Less than 1 whole	One whole	More than 1 whole

Name ______________________________ Date ______________

Comparing Fractions

Compare the shaded parts.
Write > or <.

1.  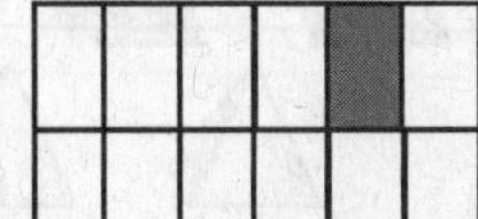

$\frac{1}{5}$  > $\frac{1}{12}$

2. 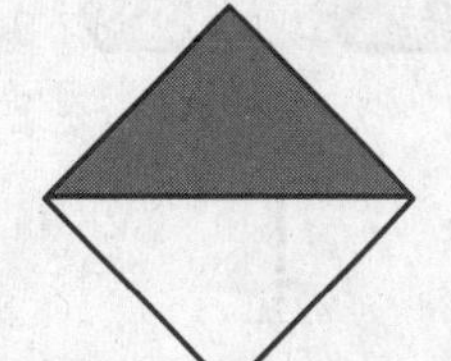 

$\frac{1}{2}$  $\frac{1}{8}$

3. 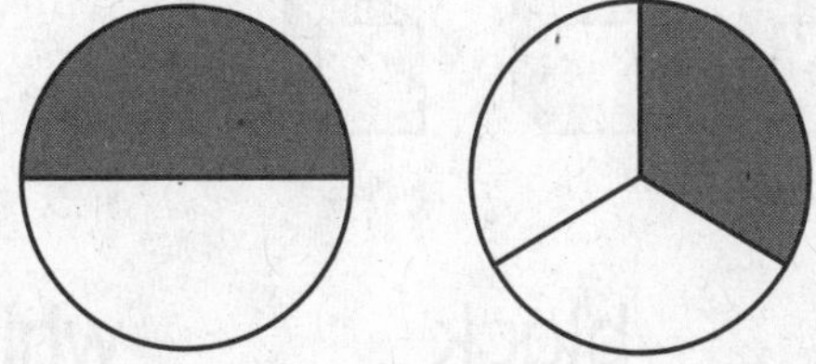

$\frac{1}{2}$ 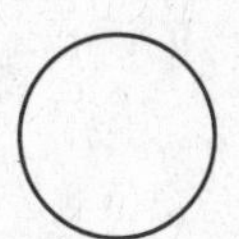 $\frac{1}{3}$

4. 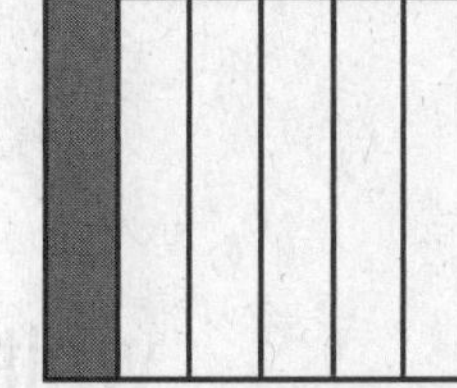 

$\frac{1}{6}$ ◯ $\frac{1}{2}$

Problem Solving • Reasoning

5. Lena ate $\frac{1}{4}$ of the pizza.
Tyrel ate $\frac{1}{3}$ of the pizza.
Who ate more pizza?

____

Draw or write to explain.

Name ______________________ Date ____________

Fractions of a Group

Write a fraction for each shaded part.

1.    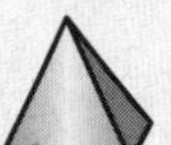 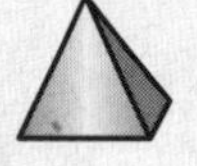

$\frac{3}{4}$ black $\frac{1}{4}$ white

2. 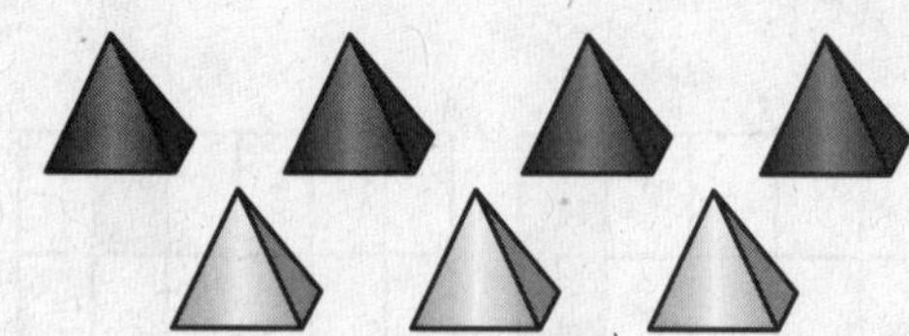

____ black ____ white

3.   

____ black ____ white

4. 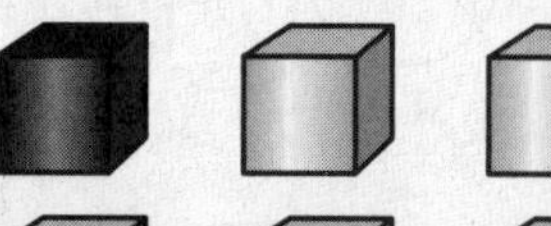

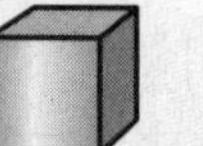  

____ black ____ white

5. 

____ black ____ white

6. 

____ black ____ white

Problem Solving • Reasoning

7. Color to show $\frac{4}{8}$ black.

Color to show $\frac{4}{8}$ red.

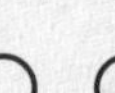 

8. Color to show $\frac{4}{10}$ black.

Color to show $\frac{6}{10}$ red.

Name ______________________ Date ____________

Fractional Parts of a Group

Color to show each fraction.
Write the number.

1. $\frac{1}{4}$

$\frac{1}{4}$ of 8 is 2.

2. $\frac{3}{5}$

$\frac{3}{5}$ of 10 is _____.

3. $\frac{1}{2}$

$\frac{1}{2}$ of 8 is _____.

4. $\frac{1}{3}$

$\frac{1}{3}$ of 12 is _____.

Problem Solving • Reasoning

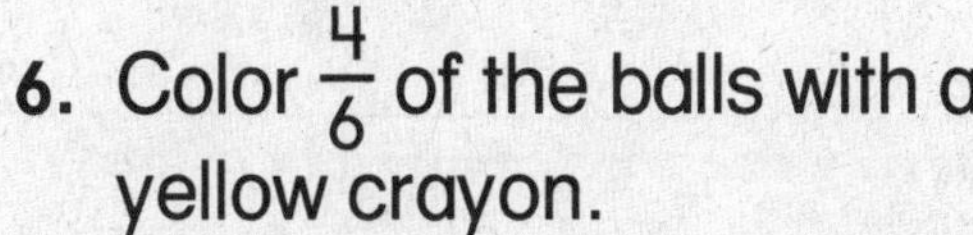

5. Color $\frac{2}{6}$ of the balls with a red crayon.

6. Color $\frac{4}{6}$ of the balls with a yellow crayon.

7. Write how many. _____ red balls _____ yellow balls

Name ______________________ Date ____________

More Likely or Less Likely

Use a pencil and a paper clip to spin the spinner.
Record the number. Repeat 9 times.

1.

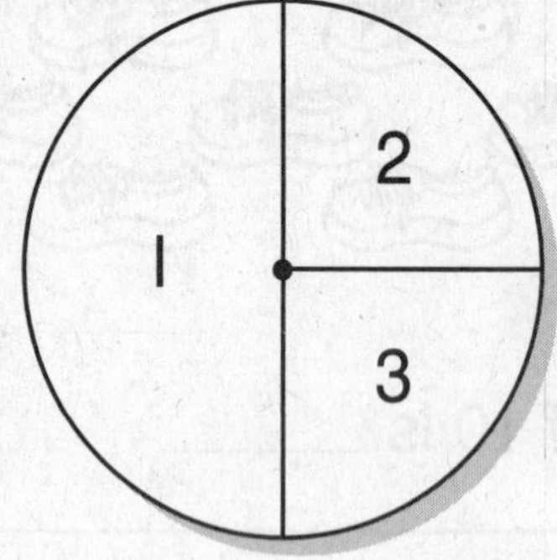

Number	Results
1	
2	
3	

Circle the number that the spinner is **most likely** to land on.

1 2 3

2.

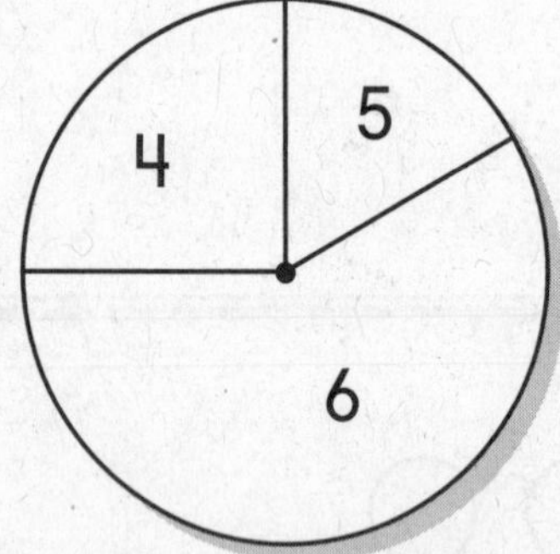

Number	Results
4	
5	
6	

Circle the number that the spinner is **most likely** to land on.

4 5 6

Name ______________________ Date ____________

Problem Solving: Use Data From a Picture

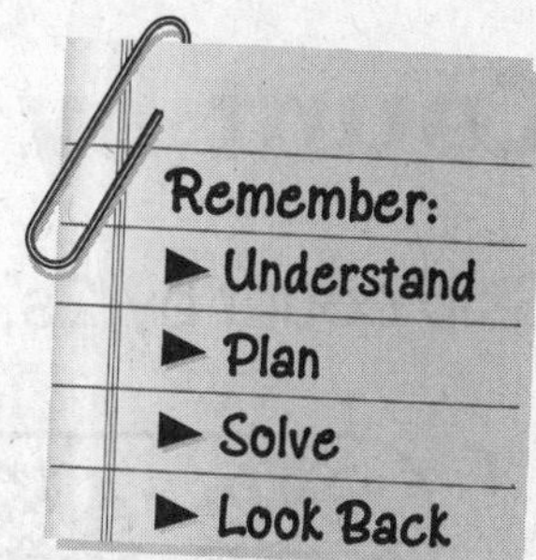

You can use information in a picture to solve a problem.

Use the picture to solve problems 1 and 2.

1. Nick gave 2 slices of pie to his sister. What fraction of the pie did he give her?

   Think: How many slices are there in all?

   _____ of the pie

   Draw or write to explain.

2. Nikki ate $\frac{2}{6}$ of the pie. Joe ate $\frac{3}{6}$ of the pie. Who ate more pie?

   Think: Which is greater, $\frac{2}{6}$ or $\frac{3}{6}$?

   _________ ate more

   Draw or write to explain.

Solve. Choose a strategy.

- Draw a picture.
- Write a number sentence.

3. Latisha cut her apple into 3 pieces. She ate 1 piece. What fraction of the apple did she eat?

   _____ of the apple

   Draw or write to explain.

Name ______________________ Date ____________

Count by Twos, Fives, and Tens

Skip count by 2s, 5s, or 10s. Write the numbers.

1.  

3 groups of 2

2, 4, 6   6 in all

2.  

6 groups of 10

____, ____, ____, ____, ____, ____   ____ in all

3.  

3 groups of 5

____, ____, ____   ____ in all

4.    

4 groups of 2

____, ____, ____, ____   ____ in all

Problem Solving • Reasoning

5. You know that 1 dime equals 10¢. If you have 5 dimes, how many cents do you have? ____¢

Name ______________________ Date ____________

Adding Equal Groups

Draw equal groups of squares. Then add.

1. 2 equal groups of 6.

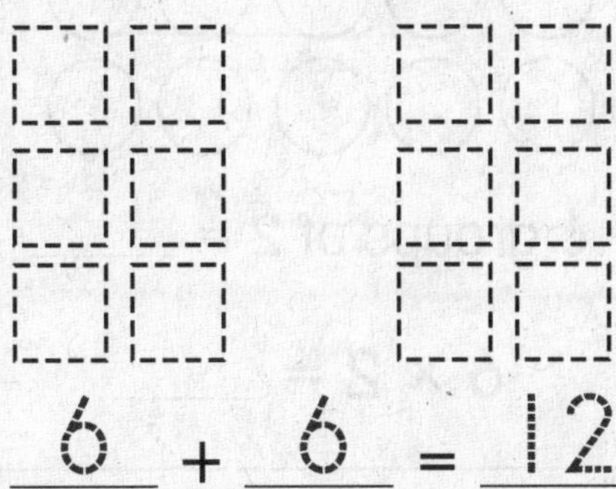

6 + 6 = 12

2. 3 equal groups of 5.

____ + ____ + ____ = ____

3. 4 equal groups of 3.

____ + ____ + ____ + ____ = ____

4. 2 equal groups of 10.

____ + ____ = ____

Problem Solving • Reasoning

Write About It

5. John wants to give his mother a bunch of 12 roses for Mother's Day. He has 4 rosebushes and each bush has 3 roses. Does John have enough roses? Explain.

yes no

Draw or write to explain.

Name ______________________ Date __________

Multiply With 2

Write how many in all. Then write the product.

1\.

4 groups of 2 = 8

4 × 2 = 8

2\.

6 groups of 2 = ____

6 × 2 = ____

3\.

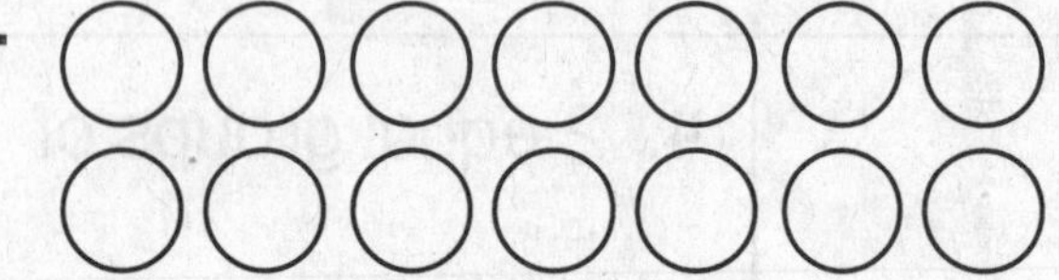

7 groups of 2 = ____

7 × 2 = ____

4\.

3 groups of 2 = ____

3 × 2 = ____

Multiply.

5\. 5 × 2 = ____ | 6. 2 × 2 = ____ | 7. 10 × 2 = ____

8\. 3 × 2 = ____ | 9. 8 × 2 = ____ | 10. 6 × 2 = ____

Problem Solving • Reasoning

11\. Jane has 2 packs of pencils. Each pack has 8 pencils in it. How many pencils does Jane have?

____ × ____ = ____

12\. Mark has 2 packs of crayons. Each pack has 6 crayons. How many crayons does Mark have?

____ × ____ = ____

Name ______________________ Date __________

Multiply With 5

Write how many in all.
Then write the multiplication sentence.

1. 

3 groups of 5 = 15

3 × 5 = 15

2. 

8 groups of 5 = _____

_____ × _____ = _____

3. 

5 groups of 5 = _____

_____ × _____ = _____

4. 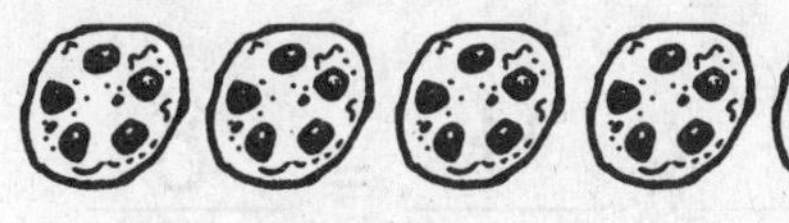

6 groups of 5 = _____

_____ × _____ = _____

Multiply.

5. 2 × 5 = _____
6. 4 × 5 = _____
7. 3 × 5 = _____

Problem Solving • Reasoning

Write About It

8. How can you use multiplication to find the total amount the coins are worth?

Name ______________________ Date __________

Algebra Readiness: Multiply in Any Order

Color in the circles to make equal rows.

Find each product.

1. 4 rows of 2 — 2 rows of 4

4 × 2 = 8

2 × 4 = 8

2. 5 rows of 3 — 3 rows of 5

____ × ____ = ____

____ × ____ = ____

Multiply.

3. 5 × 2 = ____ 2 × 5 = ____

4. 6 × 5 = ____ 5 × 6 = ____

5. 6 × 4 = ____ 4 × 6 = ____

6. 4 × 8 = ____ 8 × 4 = ____

7. 3 × 7 = ____ 7 × 3 = ____

8. 9 × 2 = ____ 2 × 9 = ____

Problem Solving • Reasoning

9. Two numbers have a product of 8 and a sum of 6. What are the numbers?

____ and ____

Draw or write to explain.

Name ______________________ Date ____________

Multiply With 10

Multiply.

1. Multiply by 2

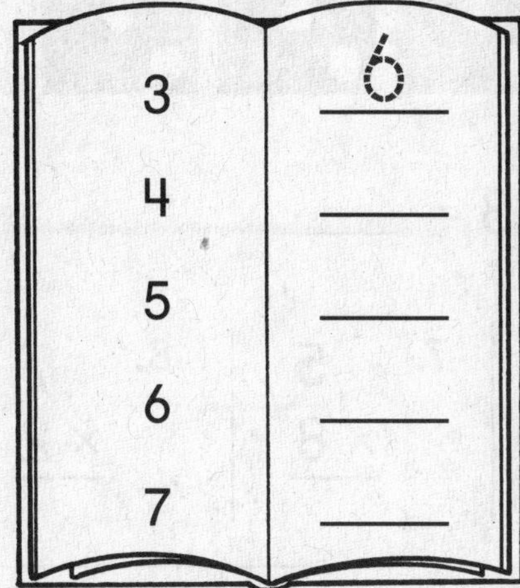

2. Multiply by 5

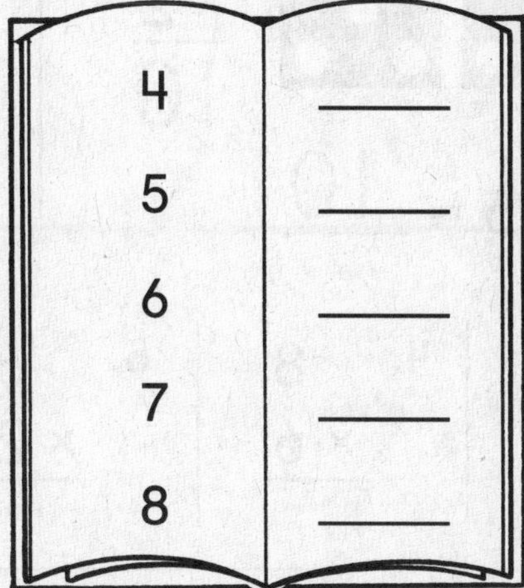

3. Multiply by 10

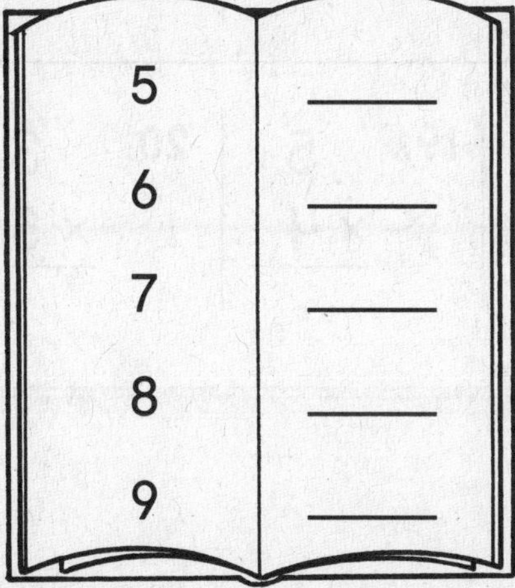

4. Multiply by 2

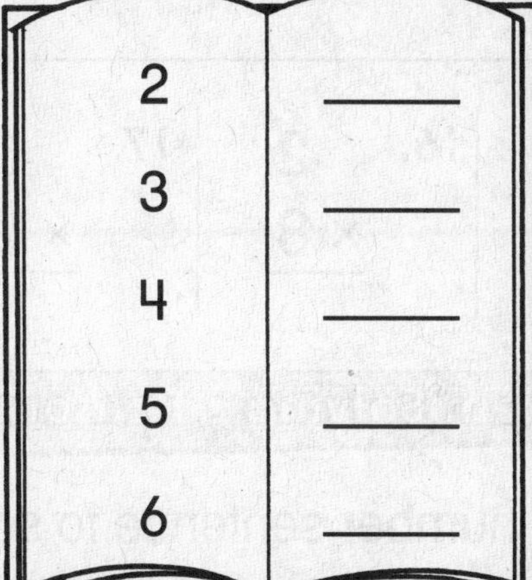

Problem Solving • Reasoning

5. You are making ice cream sundaes for 10 people. Each sundae has 4 scoops of ice cream. How many scoops do you need? _____ scoops

Name ______________________ Date __________

Multiply in Vertical Form

Find each product.

1.  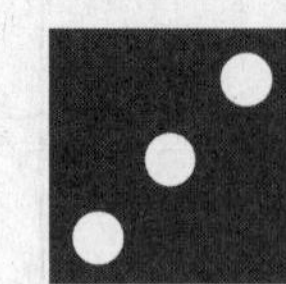

$$\begin{array}{r} 5 \\ \times 2 \\ \hline 10 \end{array}$$

$2 \times 5 =$ 10

2.   

$$\begin{array}{r} 3 \\ \times 4 \\ \hline \end{array}$$

$4 \times 3 =$ ____

3. $\begin{array}{r} 9 \\ \times 5 \\ \hline \end{array}$
4. $\begin{array}{r} 8 \\ \times 6 \\ \hline \end{array}$
5. $\begin{array}{r} 6 \\ \times 2 \\ \hline \end{array}$
6. $\begin{array}{r} 2 \\ \times 9 \\ \hline \end{array}$
7. $\begin{array}{r} 5 \\ \times 8 \\ \hline \end{array}$
8. $\begin{array}{r} 7 \\ \times 2 \\ \hline \end{array}$
9. $\begin{array}{r} 8 \\ \times 5 \\ \hline \end{array}$
10. $\begin{array}{r} 6 \\ \times 5 \\ \hline \end{array}$
11. $\begin{array}{r} 5 \\ \times 5 \\ \hline \end{array}$
12. $\begin{array}{r} 4 \\ \times 2 \\ \hline \end{array}$
13. $\begin{array}{r} 5 \\ \times 2 \\ \hline \end{array}$
14. $\begin{array}{r} 2 \\ \times 3 \\ \hline \end{array}$
15. $\begin{array}{r} 7 \\ \times 2 \\ \hline \end{array}$
16. $\begin{array}{r} 2 \\ \times 8 \\ \hline \end{array}$
17. $\begin{array}{r} 2 \\ \times 2 \\ \hline \end{array}$
18. $\begin{array}{r} 5 \\ \times 9 \\ \hline \end{array}$
19. $\begin{array}{r} 5 \\ \times 4 \\ \hline \end{array}$
20. $\begin{array}{r} 3 \\ \times 5 \\ \hline \end{array}$

Problem Solving • Reasoning

Write a number sentence to solve.

21. You have 5 planters. Each planter holds 7 tulips. How many tulips are there?

____ × ____ = ____

22. Al has 2 planters. Each planter holds 7 tulips. How many tulips can Al plant?

____ × ____ = ____

Name ______________________ Date __________

Multiply With 1 and 0

Find each product.

1.  

$4 \times 1 =$ 4

2.    

$4 \times 0 =$ 0

3. $3 \times 0 =$ ____
4. $4 \times 0 =$ ____
5. $1 \times 8 =$ ____
6. $6 \times 1 =$ ____
7. $1 \times 3 =$ ____
8. $5 \times 0 =$ ____
9. $0 \times 9 =$ ____
10. $1 \times 9 =$ ____
11. $0 \times 6 =$ ____

12. 4×1
13. 2×3
14. 9×2
15. 6×5
16. 7×5
17. 2×1

18. 7×0
19. 2×0
20. 0×9
21. 0×7
22. 2×4
23. 9×2

Problem Solving • Reasoning

24. Circle the number sentence that matches the picture.

$6 \times 1 = 6$ $6 + 1 = 7$

Name ______________________ Date ____________

Different Ways to Multiply

- Use counters.
- Draw a picture.
- Skip count.

Choose a way to solve each problem.

1. $\begin{array}{r} 1 \\ \times 9 \\ \hline 9 \end{array}$	2. $\begin{array}{r} 8 \\ \times 5 \\ \hline \end{array}$	3. $\begin{array}{r} 10 \\ \times 5 \\ \hline \end{array}$	4. $\begin{array}{r} 0 \\ \times 7 \\ \hline \end{array}$	5. $\begin{array}{r} 2 \\ \times 4 \\ \hline \end{array}$
6. $\begin{array}{r} 6 \\ \times 5 \\ \hline \end{array}$	7. $\begin{array}{r} 1 \\ \times 0 \\ \hline \end{array}$	8. $\begin{array}{r} 4 \\ \times 5 \\ \hline \end{array}$	9. $\begin{array}{r} 10 \\ \times 0 \\ \hline \end{array}$	10. $\begin{array}{r} 7 \\ \times 2 \\ \hline \end{array}$
11. $\begin{array}{r} 9 \\ \times 10 \\ \hline \end{array}$	12. $\begin{array}{r} 2 \\ \times 2 \\ \hline \end{array}$	13. $\begin{array}{r} 3 \\ \times 1 \\ \hline \end{array}$	14. $\begin{array}{r} 5 \\ \times 7 \\ \hline \end{array}$	15. $\begin{array}{r} 0 \\ \times 8 \\ \hline \end{array}$

16. $1 \times 6 =$ ____ 17. $3 \times 5 =$ ____ 18. $4 \times 2 =$ ____

Problem Solving • Reasoning

19. Each can holds 2 servings of pet food. How many servings of food does Poofie get?

_____ servings

20. **Write Your Own** Write a problem by using the information in the graph. Then solve.

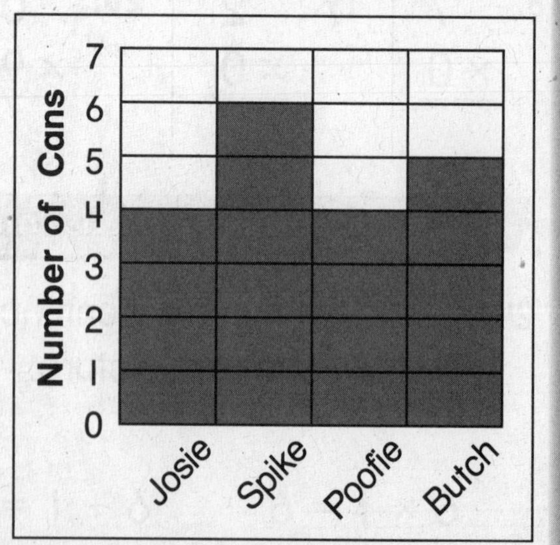

Name ____________________ Date __________

Problem Solving: Draw a Picture

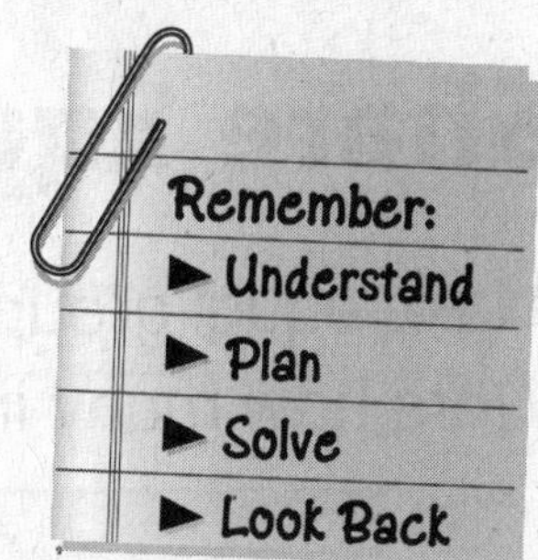

Sometimes you can draw a picture to solve a problem.

Solve each problem. Draw a picture to help you.

1. Tanya has 3 friends at camp. Each friend sends her 3 letters. How many letters does she get?

   _____ letters

   Think: What should I draw?

   Draw or write to explain.

2. Rashid did 10 math problems every day. How many math problems did he do in 3 days?

   _____ problems

   Think: How many problems did he do each day? How many days?

   Draw or write to explain.

Solve. Choose a strategy.

- Draw a picture.
- Write a number sentence.

3. There are 7 boats. Each boat has 2 sails. How many sails are there in all?

   _____ sails

   Draw or write to explain.

Name ________________________ Date ____________

Share Equally

Make equal groups of balls. Circle the groups. Write how many in each group.

	Number of Circles	Number of Equal Groups	Number in Each Group
1.	4 ○○○○	2	2
2.	6 ○○○○○○	2	____
3.	8 ○○○○○○○○	4	____
4.	16 ○○○○○○○○○○○○○○○○	4	____
5.	14 ○○○○○○○○○○○○○○	2	____
6.	6 ○○○○○○	3	____
7.	10 ○○○○○○○○○○	2	____
8.	18 ○○○○○○○○○○○○○○○○○○	2	____

Problem Solving • Reasoning

Draw to show equal groups.

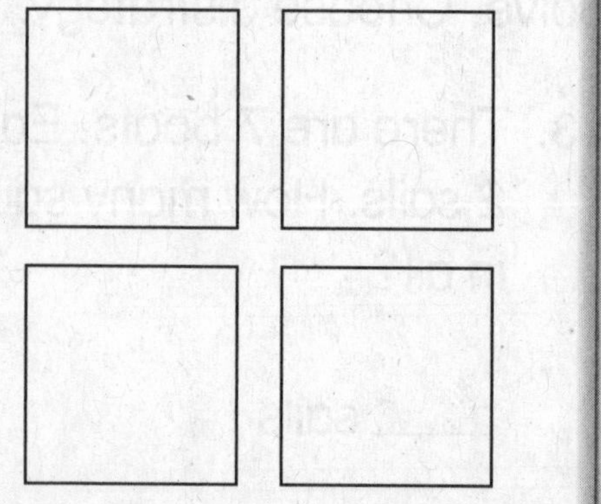

9. Four children share a bag of 20 peanuts equally. How many peanuts does each child get?

____ peanuts

Name ______________________ Date ____________

Equal Groups of 2

Circle equal groups of 2. Write the number of groups.

1. 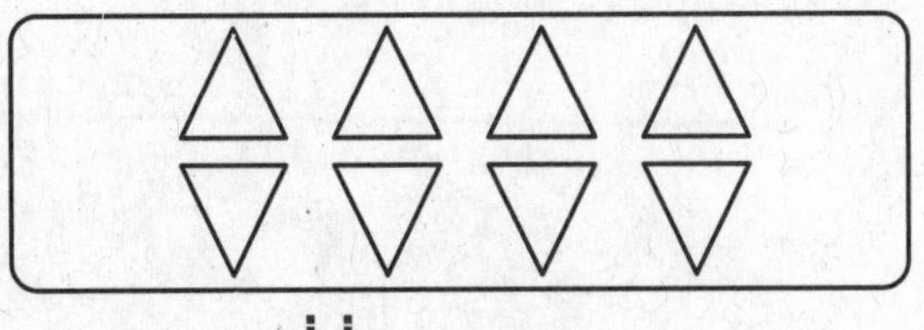

$8 \div 2 =$ 4 groups.

2. 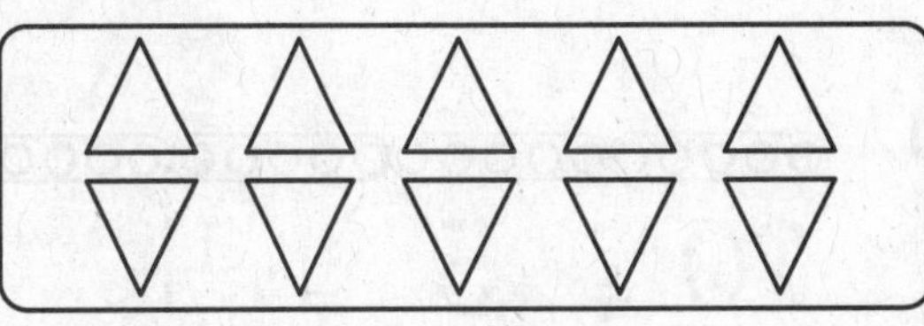

$10 \div 2 =$ ____ groups.

3. 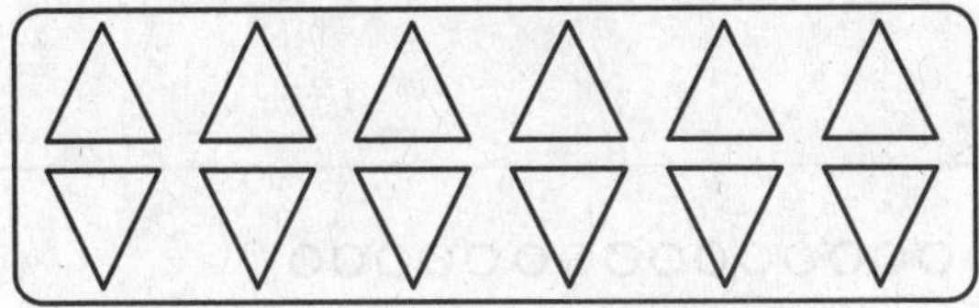

$12 \div 2 =$ ____ groups.

4. 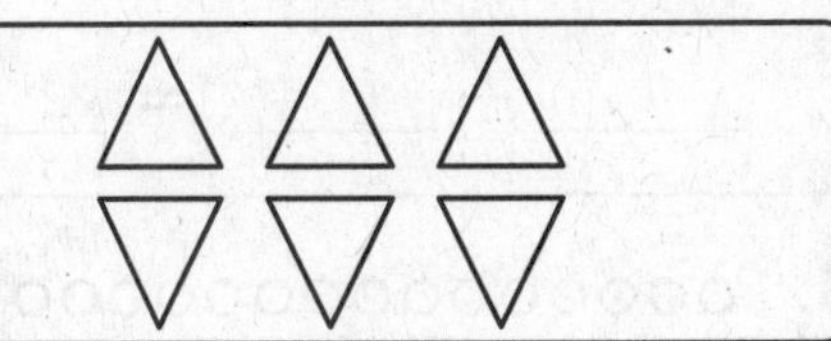

$6 \div 2 =$ ____ groups.

Problem Solving • Reasoning

5. How many flowers were planted on Thursday?

____ flowers

6. Use the information from the pictograph to write a story problem. Then solve.

Flowers Planted	
Monday	✿ ✿
Tuesday	✿
Wednesday	✿ ✿ ✿
Thursday	✿ ✿
Friday	✿ ✿ ✿ ✿

Each ✿ stands for 2 flowers.

Name ______________________ Date ____________

Equal Groups of 5

Circle groups of five dots. Then write the division sentence.

1. ○○○○○○○○○○○○○○○○○○○○

20 ÷ 5 = 4

2. ○○○○○○○○○○○○○○○ ○○○○○○○○○○ ○○○○○○○○○○

____ ÷ ____ = ____

3. ○○○○○○○○○○○○○○○ ○○○○○○○○○○ ○○○○○○○○○○○○○○○

____ ÷ ____ = ____

4. ○○○○○○○○○○○○○○○

____ ÷ ____ = ____

5. ○○○○○○○○○○○○○○○ ○○○○○○○○○○ ○○○○○○○○○○ ○○○○○○○○○○○○○○○

____ ÷ ____ = ____

Problem Solving • Reasoning

6. Jack has 15 muffins. He wants to share them equally among three people. Circle the picture that shows how he should divide.

Name ______________________ Date ____________

Equal Groups With Remainders

Write each division sentence. Write the remainder.

	Start with this many.	Number of equal groups	Complete the division sentence.
1.	10	5	10 ÷ 5 = 2 remainder 0
2.	12	5	12 ÷ 5 = ___ remainder ___
3.	10	6	10 ÷ 6 = ___ remainder ___
4.	9	4	9 ÷ 4 = ___ remainder ___
5.	9	2	9 ÷ 2 = ___ remainder ___
6.	12	8	12 ÷ 8 = ___ remainder ___
7.	9	3	9 ÷ 3 = ___ remainder ___
8.	10	4	10 ÷ 4 = ___ remainder ___

Problem Solving • Reasoning

Circle the division sentence that shows the answer to the problem.

9. Five people share a bag of carrots. There are 20 carrots in the bag. Each person gets an equal number of carrots. How many carrots will each person get?

20 ÷ 4 = 5 20 ÷ 5 = 4 30 − 10 = 20 10 + 10 = 20

Name ____________________ Date __________

Problem Solving: Choose the Operation

You may need to add, subtract, or multiply to solve a problem.

Solve. Add, subtract or multiply.

1. Jamal's team scored 17 points in the first game and 18 points in the second game. How many points did they score in all?

Think: Am I finding how many in all or am I comparing?

Draw or write to explain.

_____ ◯ _____ = _____ points

2. Each tank has 8 dolphins. If there are 3 tanks, how many dolphins are there?

Think: How many groups are there? Are the groups equal?

Draw or write to explain.

_____ ◯ _____ = _____ dolphins

Solve. Choose a strategy.

- Draw a picture.
- Write a number sentence.

3. 25 second graders brought peanut butter sandwiches for lunch. 9 second graders brought tuna fish sandwiches. How many more peanut butter sandwiches were there?

Draw or write to explain.

_____ more peanut butter sandwiches

Name ______________________ Date ____________

Nonstandard Units

Use the unit shown.
Estimate. Then measure.

1.

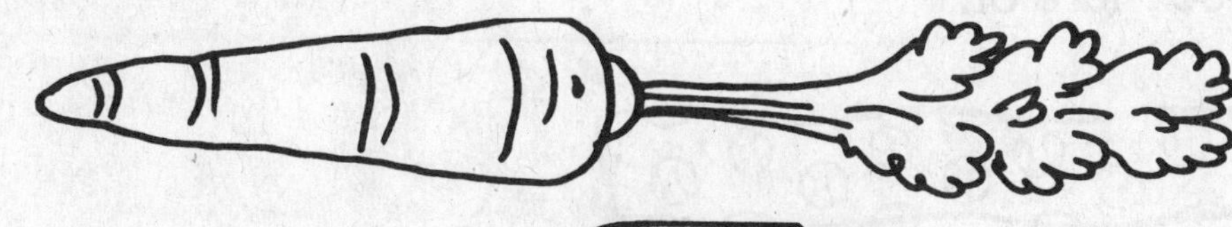

Estimate: about 4

Measure: about 4

2.

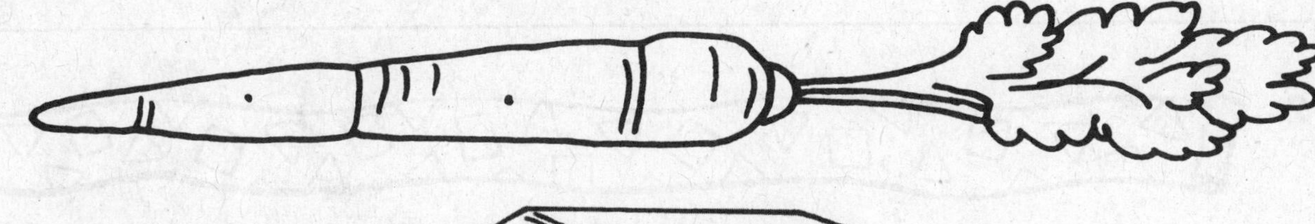

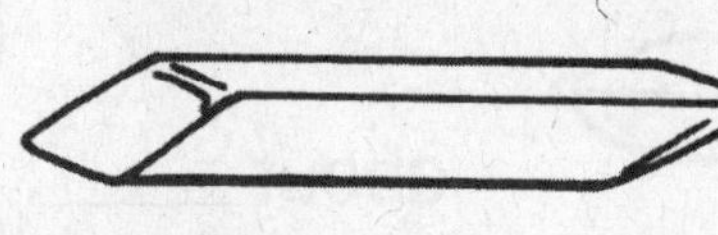

Estimate: about ____

Measure: about ____

Problem Solving • Reasoning

Eve, Scott, Jim, and Joan measure the length of their kitchen by taking steps.

Eve: 20 steps

Scott: 22 steps

Jim: 25 steps

Joan: 19 steps

3. Who takes the longest step?

____

4. Who takes the shortest step?

____

Name ______________________ Date ____________

Compare Nonstandard Units

Measure with . Then measure with 

.

Circle the unit you use more of.

1. 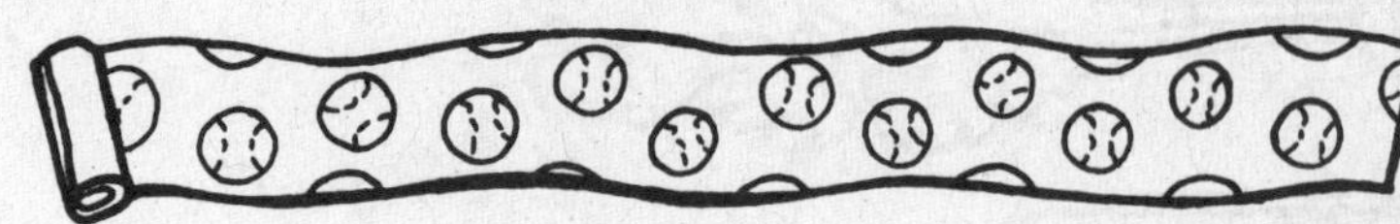

about 3 about 4 

2. 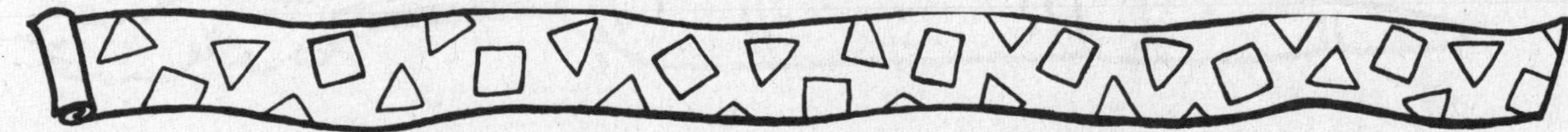

about _____ about _____ 

Problem Solving • Reasoning

Mr. Tubb asked the children to measure a table with these units.

 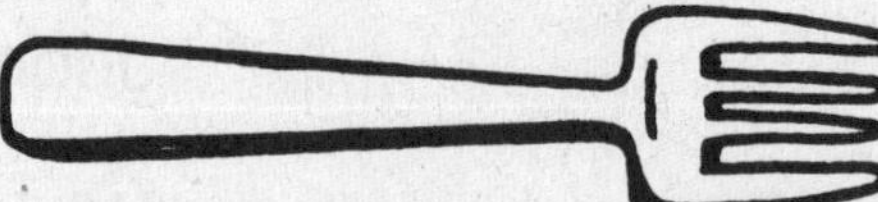

3. Which unit will they use more of? ______________

4. How do you know? ______________

Name ______________________ Date ____________

Inches and Feet

Remember: 12 inches = 1 foot.

About how long or tall is each real object?
Circle the better estimate.

1. 
7 inches long
7 feet long

2. 
10 inches long
10 feet long

3. 
6 inches long
6 feet long

4. 
1 inch tall
1 foot tall

5. 
2 inches tall
2 feet tall

6. 

10 inches tall
10 feet tall

Problem Solving • Reasoning

7. Laura and Rod measure the height of a table. Laura says it is 2 feet high and Rod says it is 24 inches high. Who is correct? How do you know?

Name ______________________ Date ____________

Centimeters and Meters

About how long or tall is each real object?
Circle the better estimate.

1. 

2 cm long

2 meters long

2. 

10 cm tall

10 m tall

3. 

8 cm long

8 m long

4. 

2 cm tall

2 m tall

5. 

7 cm long

7 m long

6. 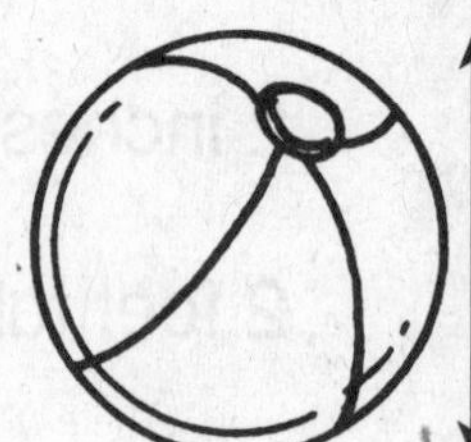

12 cm tall

12 m tall

Problem Solving • Reasoning

7. Circle the correct way to measure the length of the paper clip.

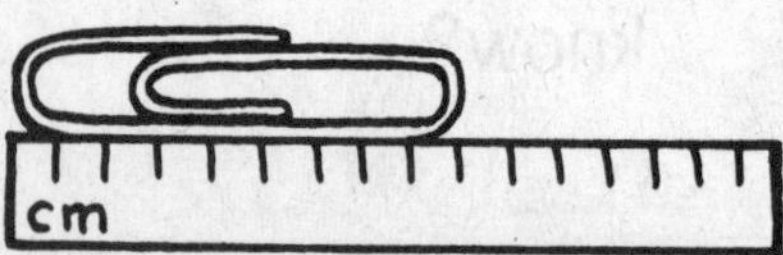

Name ______________________ Date ______________

Perimeter

Measure each side.
Add to find the total.

1.  4 + 2 + 4 + 2 = 12 cm

2. 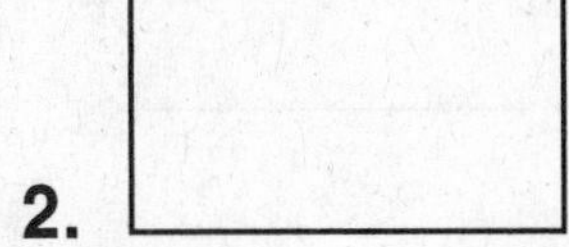 ____ + ____ + ____ + ____ = ____ cm

3. 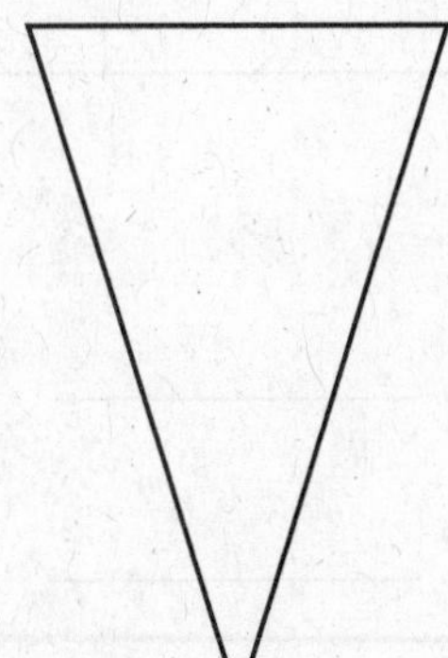 ____ + ____ + ____ = ____ cm

Problem Solving • Reasoning

4. Cliff's mother told him he could plant flowers around the perimeter of the backyard. What is the perimeter?

9 m
4 m 4 m
9 m

____ meters

5. **Write About It** Explain how you found the perimeter.

Name ______________________ Date __________

Problem Solving: Guess and Check

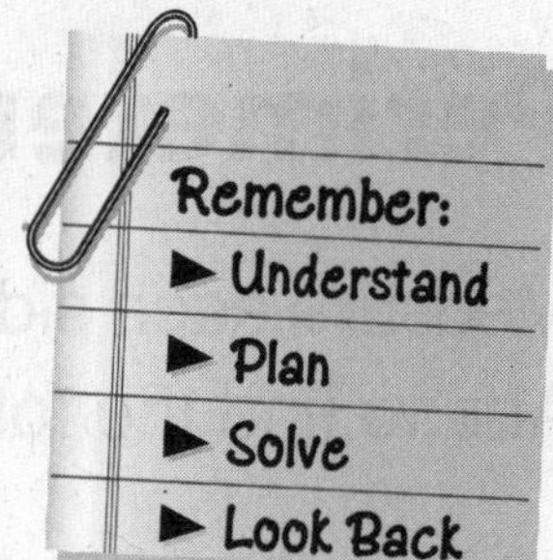

You can cover a shape with square units to find how many will fit.

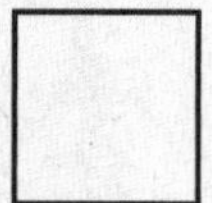

How many square units will cover the shape? Guess. Then measure to check.

1. 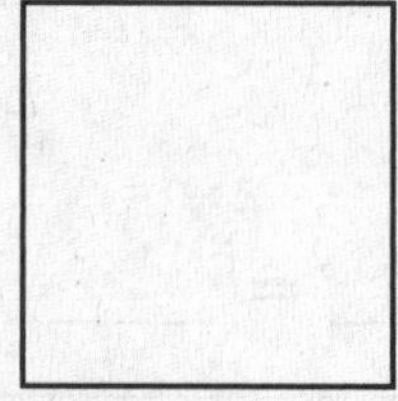

Think: How can the size of the square units help me make a guess?

Guess: __________

Check: __________

2. 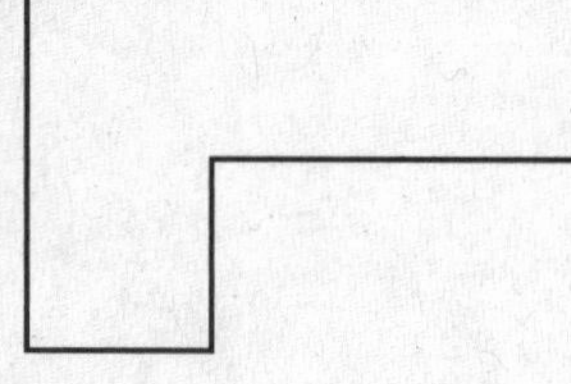

Think: What will help me make a guess?

Guess: __________

Check: __________

Solve. Choose a strategy.

- Guess and check.
- Write a number sentence.

3. Marta is making a quilt. Each row has 6 squares. How many squares will she need for 2 rows?

_____ squares

Draw or write to explain.

Name ______________________ Date ____________

Cups, Pints, and Quarts

Write how many cups, pints, or quarts.
Remember that 2 cups = 1 pint; 2 pints = 1 quart;
4 cups = 1 quart.

1. 4 [1 QUART] = 8 [1 PINT]
2. 8 [1 CUP] = ____ [1 PINT]
3. 4 [1 PINT] = ____ [1 QUART]
4. 16 [1 CUP] = ____ [1 QUART]
5. 3 [1 QUART] = ____ [1 CUP]
6. 5 [1 PINT] = ____ [1 CUP]
7. 5 [1 QUART] = ____ [1 PINT]
8. 2 [1 QUART] = ____ [1 PINT]

Problem Solving • Reasoning

9. The children bring water for the greenhouse garden.

Kurt brings 3 pints.

Ryan brings 7 cups.

Mary brings 2 quarts.

Who brings the most? ____________

Who brings the least? ____________

Name ______________________ Date ____________

Liters

Put an X on the objects that hold less than 1 liter.
Circle the objects that hold more than 1 liter.

1. 

2. 

3. 

4. 

5. 

6. 

7. 

8. 

9. 

Problem Solving • Reasoning

10. Circle the container that holds enough apple juice for the whole class.

11. Circle if it is more or less than a liter.

more than a liter   less than a liter

Name ______________________ Date ____________

Temperature

Write each temperature.

1. 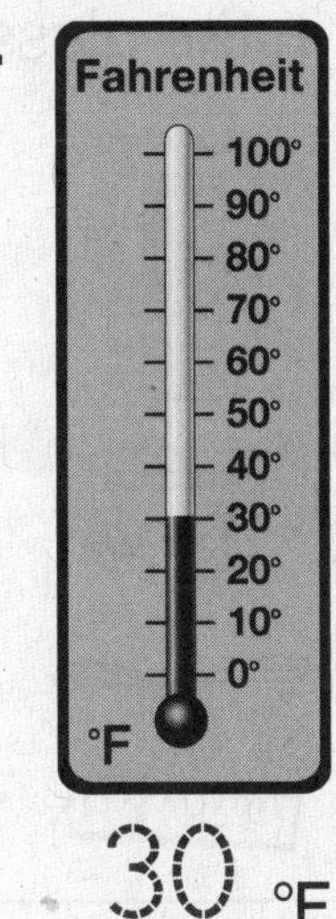

30 °F

2. 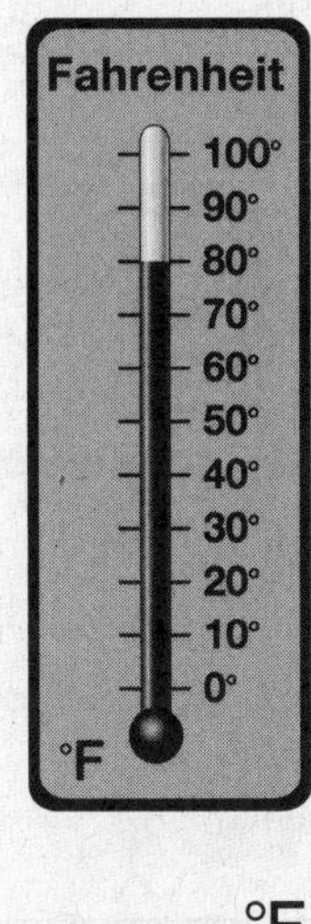

______ °F

3. 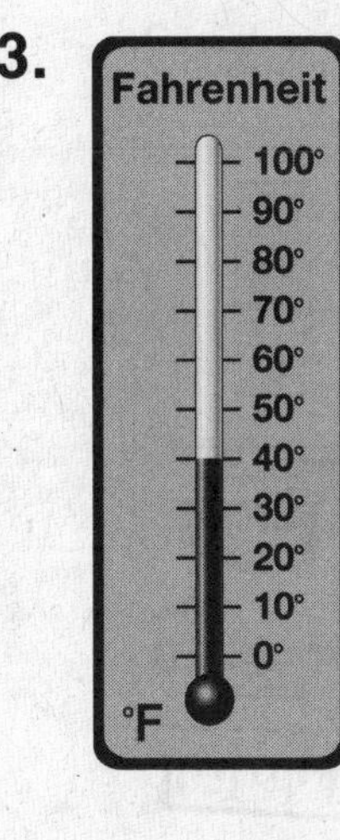

______ °F

4. 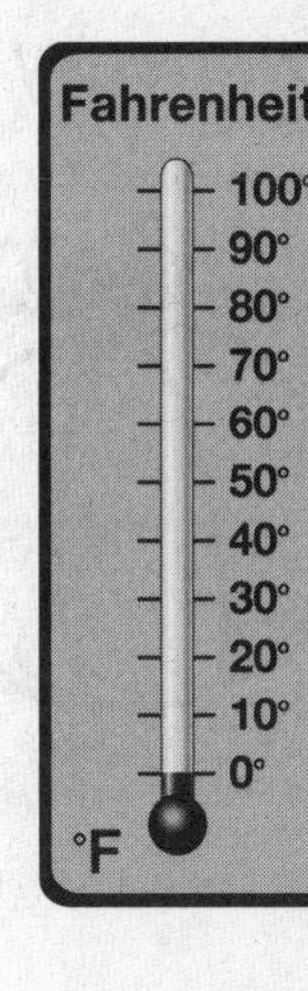

______ °F

5. 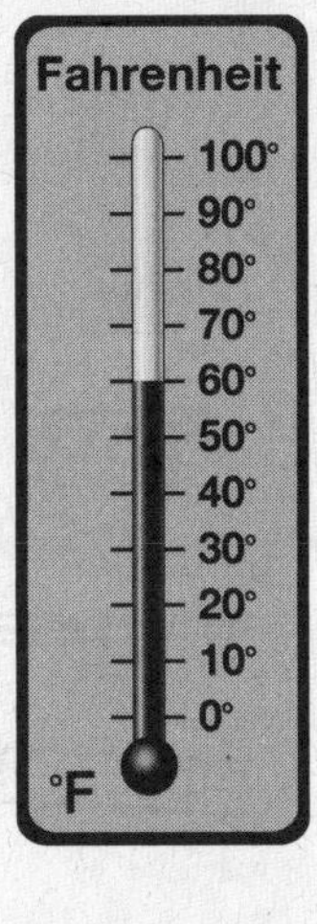

______ °F

6. 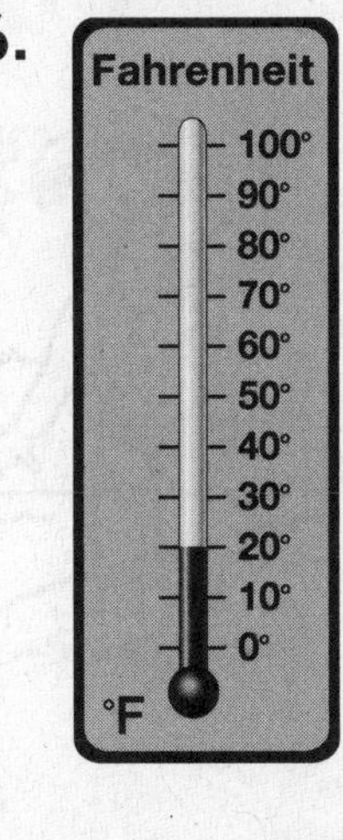

______ °F

7. 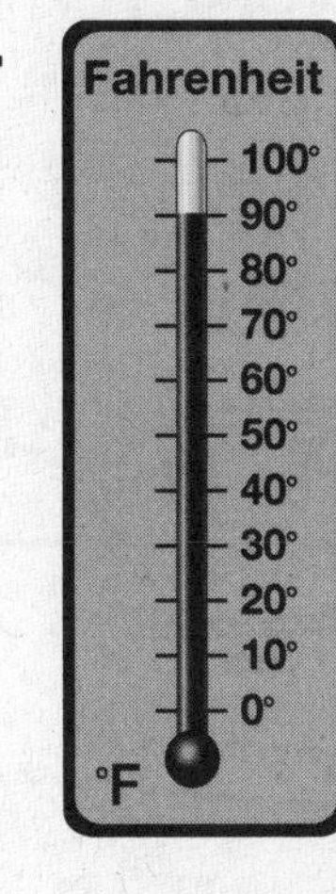

______ °F

8. 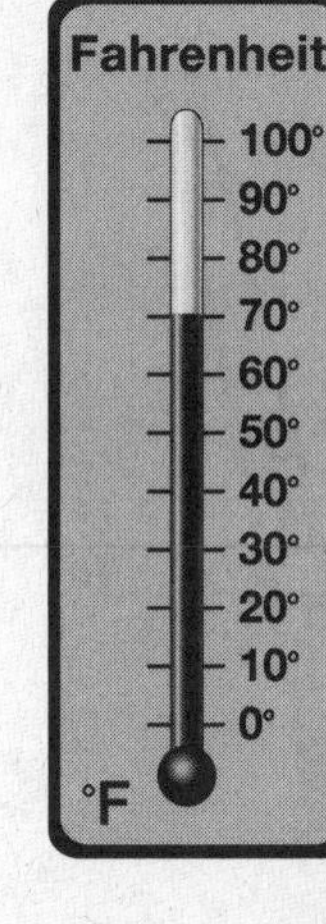

______ °F

Problem Solving • Reasoning

Temperature at Noon	
Shade	75 °F
Sun	90 °F

9. How many degrees difference is there between the temperature in the shade and the temperature in the sun? __________

Name ______________________________ Date ______________

Measurement Units and Tools

Circle the tool you would use to measure.

1. How heavy is the pumpkin?

2. How much juice is in the glass?

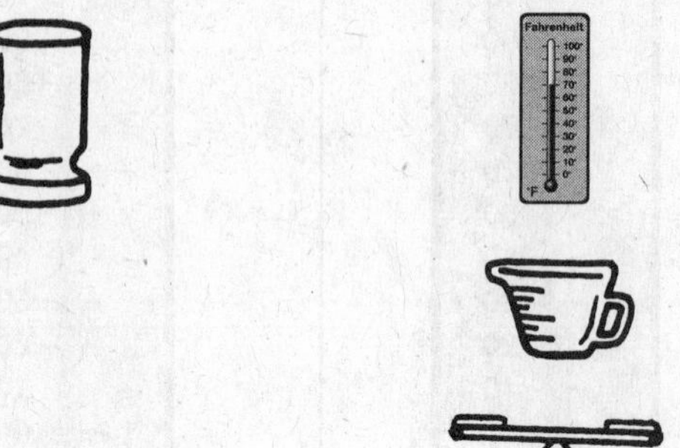

3. How long is the flute?

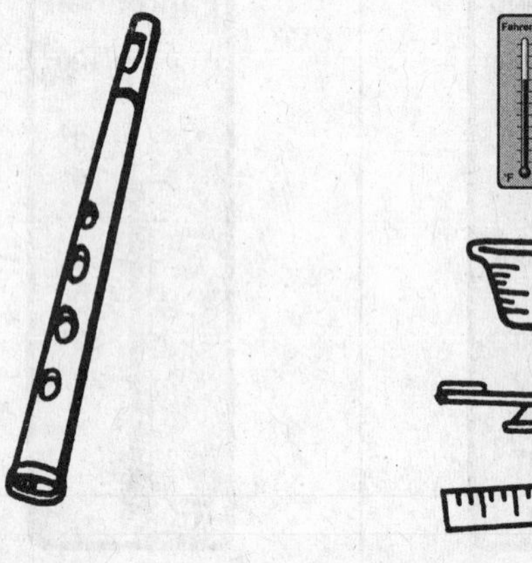

4. How hot is it?

Problem Solving • Reasoning

5. Draw a picture of something you would measure with each of the tools.

Name ______________________ Date ____________

Problem Solving: Use Measurement

You can measure to find the length of a path that is not straight.

How long is the path? Use a ruler to measure. Use a string if you need to.

1.

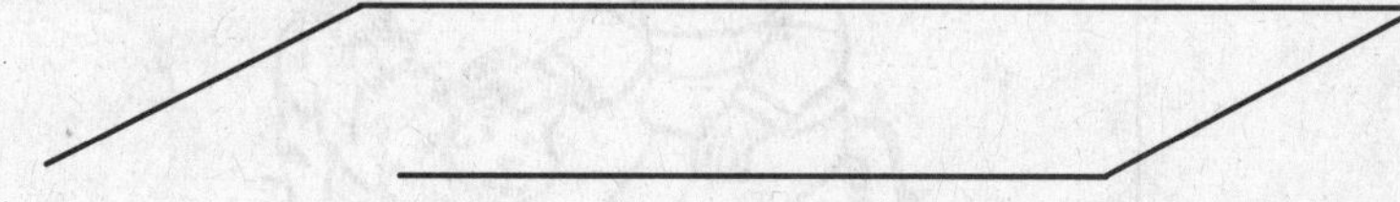

Think: About how long is each part?

____ + ____ + ____ + ____ = ____ inches

2.

Think: What will help me make a guess?

____ + ____ + ____ = ____ inches

Solve. Choose a strategy.

- Draw a picture.
- Write a number sentence.

3. Jess has two equal pieces of ribbon. The total length of both ribbons is 10 inches. How long is each ribbon?

Draw or write to explain.

____ inches

Name ______________________ Date ____________

What Is a Minute?

Will the activity take more or less than 1 minute?
Circle your answer.

1. Play soccer.

more less

2. Pet a cat.

more less

3. Play a computer game.

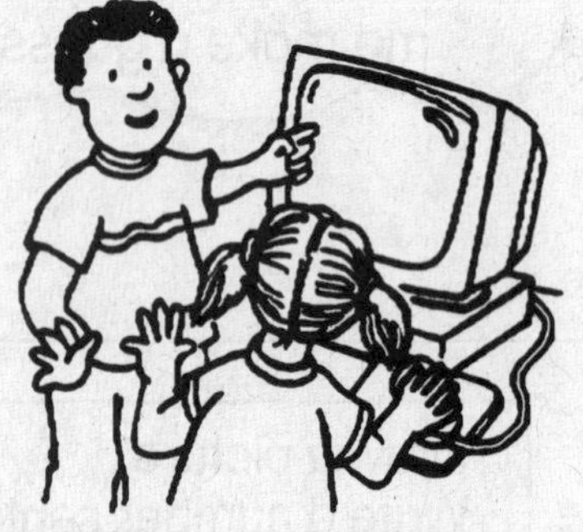

more less

4. Eat a cracker.

more less

Problem Solving • Reasoning

5. Draw a picture to show something you do that takes **less** than one minute.

6. Draw a picture to show something you do that takes **more** than one minute.

Name ______________________ Date ____________

Time to the Hour

Write the time.

1. 
2:00

2. 
___ : ___

3. 
___ : ___

4. 
___ : ___

5. 
___ : ___

6. 
___ : ___

7. 
___ : ___

8. 
___ : ___

Problem Solving • Reasoning

9. Write each time. Then label the clocks 1–4 from the earliest to the latest time shown. Hint: Start with 2:00.

___ : ___ ___ : ___ ___ : ___ ___ : ___

______ ______ ______ ______

Name ______________________ Date __________

Time to the Half-Hour

Write the time.

1. 

5:30

2. 

___:___

3. 

___:___

4. 

___:___

5. 

___:___

6. 

___:___

7. 

___:___

8. 

___:___

Problem Solving • Reasoning

9. Laura watches her favorite video tape for a half-hour. Then she reads a story for a half-hour. How long does it take her to finish both activities?

_____ minutes

10. What is another way to write this amount of time?

_____ hour

Name ______________________ Date ____________

Time to Five Minutes

Write each time.

1. 

2:45

2. 

___ : ___

3. 

___ : ___

4. 

___ : ___

Draw the minute hand to show each time.

5. 

4:35

6. 

1:55

7. 

8:45

8. 

2:00

Problem Solving • Reasoning

Look for a pattern. Write the times.

9.   

2:00 | 2:05 | 2:10 | ___ : ___ | ___ : ___

10.    

8:35 | 8:40 | 8:45 | ___ : ___ | ___ : ___

Use with text pages 469–470.

Name ______________________ Date ____________

Time to 15 Minutes

Write the time.

1. 

5:15

2. 

___ : ___

3. 

___ : ___

4. 

___ : ___

Draw the minute hand to show each time.

5. 

1:45

6. 

6:00

7. 

11:30

8. 

1:15

Problem Solving • Reasoning

Write a word that completes each sentence.

quarter-hour
half-hour
hour

9. There are 30 minutes in a ______________.

10. There are 15 minutes in a ______________.

11. There are 60 minutes in an ______________.

Name ______________________ Date __________

Elapsed Time

Write the times.
Find out how much time has passed.

A.M. is used for the hours between 12 midnight and 12 noon.
P.M. is used for the hours between 12 noon and 12 midnight.

Activity	Start	End	How much time passed?
1.	11:00 A.M.	1:00 P.M.	2 hours passed
2.	___:___ P.M.	___:___ P.M.	______ hours passed
3.	___:___ A.M.	___:___ P.M.	______ hours passed
4.	___:___ P.M.	___:___ P.M.	______ hours passed
5.	___:___ P.M.	___:___ P.M.	______ hours passed

Name ______________________ Date ____________

Problem Solving: Use Models to Act It Out

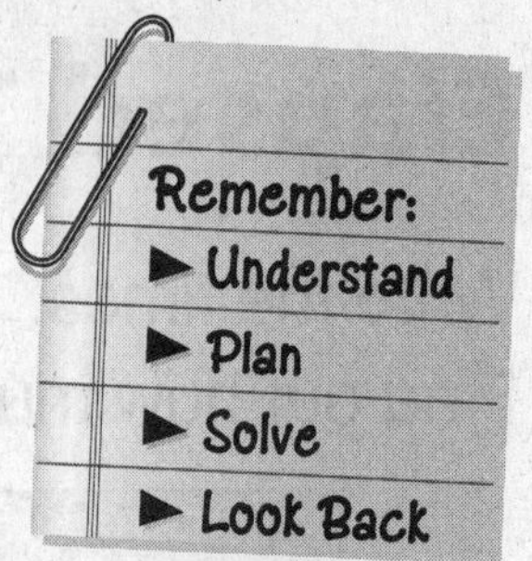

Use a clock to solve each problem. Draw the hands for the end time. Then write the time.

1. Erin goes to the beach at 9:30. She stays for 3 hours and 30 minutes. When does she leave?

Start  End 

Think: How long does she stay?

____ : ____

---

2. Basketball practice starts at 10:00. It lasts 1 hour and 30 minutes. What time is it over?

____ : ____

Solve. Choose a strategy.

- Use models to act it out.
- Write a number sentence.

3. Tamara starts playing piano at 2:30. She plays for an hour. Then she goes outside for a half-hour. What time is it when she comes in?

____ : ____

Name ______________________ Date ____________

Calendar

JANUARY

Sunday	Monday	Tuesday	Wednesday	Thursday	Friday	Saturday
			1	2	3	4
5	6	7	8	9	10	11
12	13	14	15	16	17	18
19	20	21	22	23	24	25
26	27	28	29	30	31	

FEBRUARY

Sunday	Monday	Tuesday	Wednesday	Thursday	Friday	Saturday
						1
2	3	4	5	6	7	8
9	10	11	12	13	14	15
16	17	18	19	20	21	22
23	24	25	26	27	28	

MARCH

Sunday	Monday	Tuesday	Wednesday	Thursday	Friday	Saturday
						1
2	3	4	5	6	7	8
9	10	11	12	13	14	15
16	17	18	19	20	21	22
23/30	24/31	25	26	27	28	29

APRIL

Sunday	Monday	Tuesday	Wednesday	Thursday	Friday	Saturday
		1	2	3	4	5
6	7	8	9	10	11	12
13	14	15	16	17	18	19
20	21	22	23	24	25	26
27	28	29	30			

MAY

Sunday	Monday	Tuesday	Wednesday	Thursday	Friday	Saturday
				1	2	3
4	5	6	7	8	9	10
11	12	13	14	15	16	17
18	19	20	21	22	23	24
25	26	27	28	29	30	31

JUNE

Sunday	Monday	Tuesday	Wednesday	Thursday	Friday	Saturday
1	2	3	4	5	6	7
8	9	10	11	12	13	14
15	16	17	18	19	20	21
22	23	24	25	26	27	28
29	30					

JULY

Sunday	Monday	Tuesday	Wednesday	Thursday	Friday	Saturday
		1	2	3	4	5
6	7	8	9	10	11	12
13	14	15	16	17	18	19
20	21	22	23	24	25	26
27	28	29	30	31		

AUGUST

Sunday	Monday	Tuesday	Wednesday	Thursday	Friday	Saturday
					1	2
3	4	5	6	7	8	9
10	11	12	13	14	15	16
17	18	19	20	21	22	23
24/31	25	26	27	28	29	30

Use the calendar to answer the questions.

1. Which is the first month of the year? ____________
2. Which month has fewer than 30 days? ____________
3. What date follows June 30? ____________
4. What is the third month of the year? ____________

Problem Solving • Reasoning

5. March 31 is a Monday. Explain how you can tell what day of the week April 1 will be.

Draw or write to explain.

Name ______________________________ Date ______________

Hours, Days, Weeks, Months

Circle the best way to measure each activity.

1. Bake a pie.

hours

months

2. Play a soccer game.

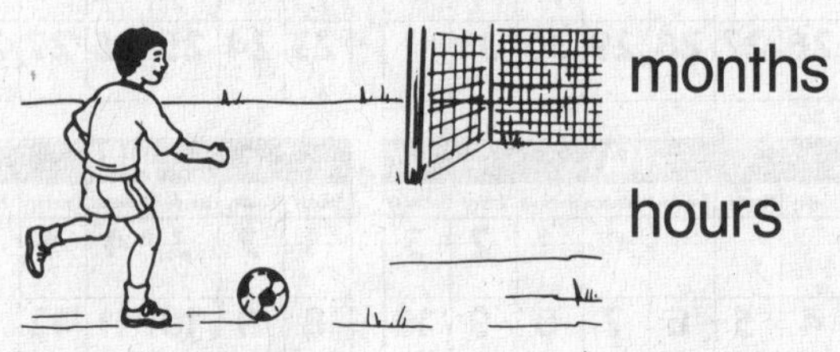

months

hours

3. Build a house.

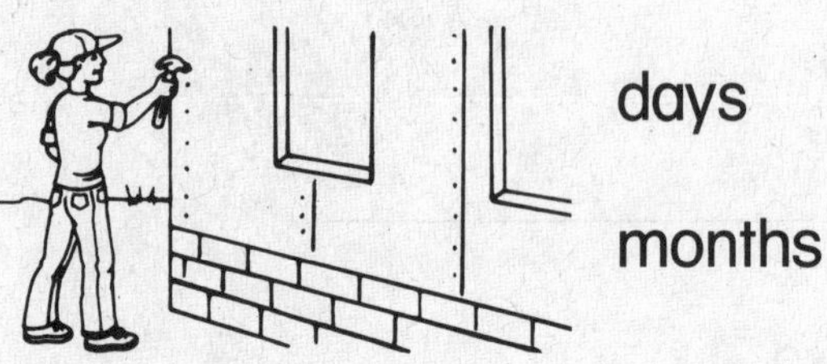

days

months

4. Learn to swim.

weeks

hours

Problem Solving • Reasoning

5. I am less than the number of days in a month. I am greater than the number of weeks in a month. What number am I? ______

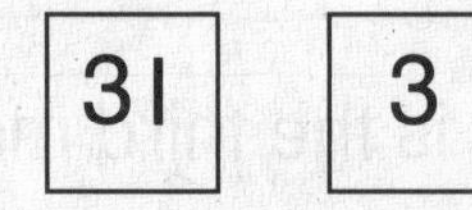

6. **Write Your Own** Write a riddle using information about hours, days, weeks, or months. Ask a friend to solve it.

Name ______________________ Date ____________

Problem Solving: Use a Schedule

Summer Camp	
Time	**Event**
9:30–10:30	Story Hour
10:30–11:30	Basketball
11:30–12:00	Sing-a-long
12:00–12:30	Lunch

Solve. Use the schedule card.

1. How long does the basketball game last?

Think: What time does the game begin?

_____ minutes

Draw or write to explain.

2. After story hour, Mrs. Tan takes the books back to the library. It takes her 30 minutes to get there. What time does she get to the library? _____ : _____

Think: What time does story hour end?

Draw or write to explain.

Solve. Choose a strategy.

- Write a number sentence.
- Draw a picture.

3. Everyone is hungry! How long does lunch last?

_____ minutes

Draw or write to explain.

Name ______________________ Date ____________

Count by 100s

Count the hundreds. Write the numbers.

1. 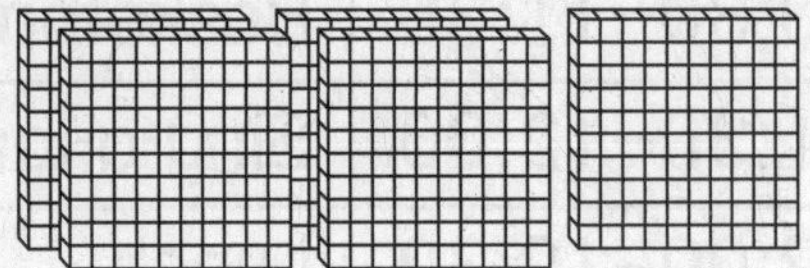

5 hundreds 500

2. 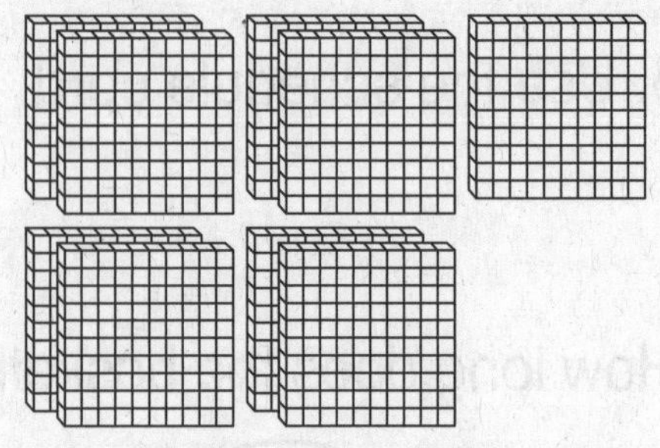

_____ hundreds _____

3. 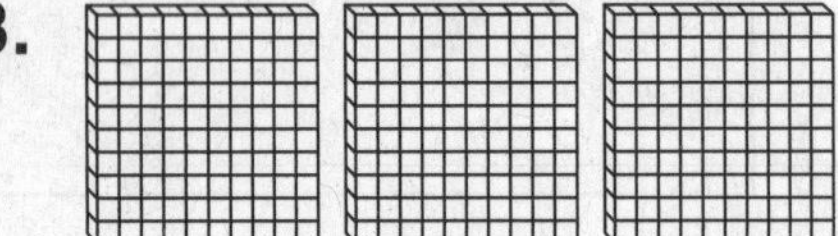

_____ hundreds _____

4. 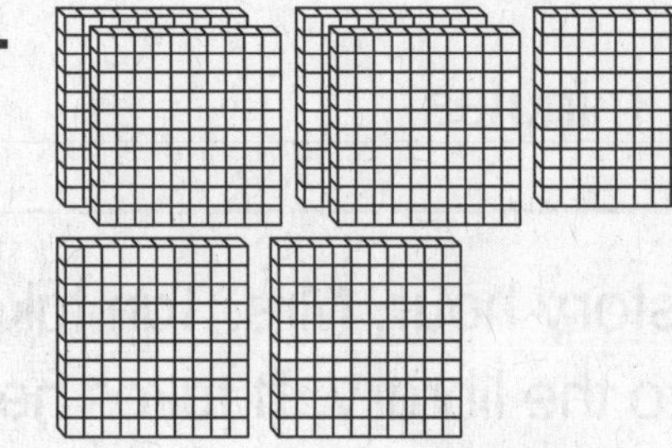

_____ hundreds _____

Write the missing numbers.

5. 100, _____, 300, 400, _____, _____, 700, _____, 900, _____

6. 1,000, _____, 800, 700, _____, 500, _____, 300, 200, _____

Problem Solving • Reasoning

7. How is 50 different from 500?
Draw a picture to show each number.

Draw or write to explain.

Name ______________________ Date ______________

Hundreds, Tens, Ones

Use Workmat 4 with blocks.

	Show this many.	Write how many hundreds, tens, and ones.	Write the number.
1.	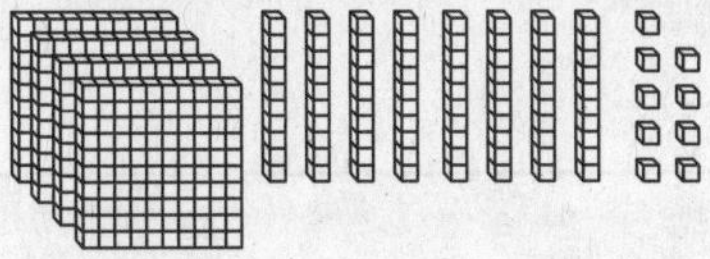	Hundreds: 4, Tens: 8, Ones: 9	489 four hundred eighty-nine
2.	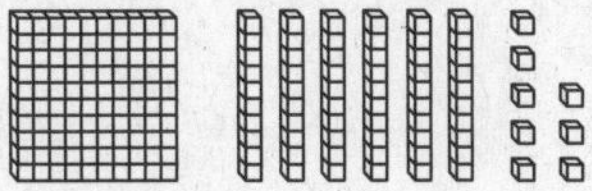	Hundreds: ___, Tens: ___, Ones: ___	______ one hundred sixty-eight
3.	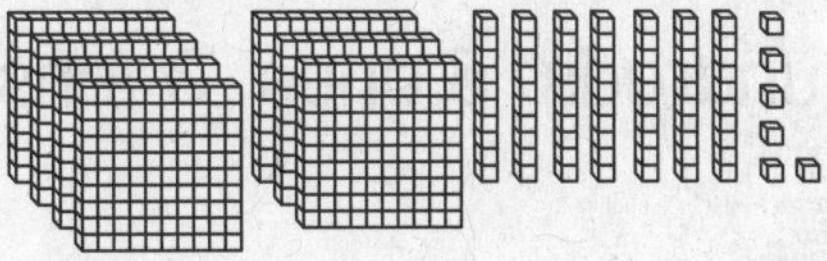	Hundreds: ___, Tens: ___, Ones: ___	______ seven hundred seventy-six

Write the missing numbers.

4. 310, ______, 330, 340, ______, 360, ______, 380, 390, ______.

5. 531, 532, ______, ______, 535, ______, 537, 538, ______, 540.

Problem Solving • Reasoning

Circle the best answer.

6. I eat breakfast __?__ times each year.

   3 30 300

7. I brush my teeth about __?__ times a day.

   3 30 300

Name ______________________ Date ____________

Numbers Through 500

Decide how many hundreds, tens, and ones there are.
Write the number.

1. 3 ones 4 hundreds 5 tens
453

2. 7 tens 4 ones 2 hundreds
____

3. 3 hundreds 1 one 0 tens
____

4. 8 tens 4 hundreds 4 ones
____

5. 4 ones 3 hundreds 9 tens
____

6. 3 hundreds 5 ones 3 tens
____

Write the missing numbers.

7. 471, 472, ____, 474, ____, ____, 477, 478, ____, ____

8. 250, ____, ____, 280, 290, ____, 310, 320, ____, ____

Problem Solving • Reasoning

9. How many ▢ in 4? ____

How many ▢ in 40? ____

How many ▢ in 400? ____

10. How many ▢ in 2? ____

How many ▢ in 20? ____

How many ▢ in 200? ____

Name ______________________ Date ____________

Numbers Through 1,000

1. Write the missing numbers.

931	932	933	934			937		939	
		943		945	946		948		
	952		954		956	957		959	
961	962			965			968	969	
			974	975		977			980
981		983	984				988		990
	992				996	997			1,000

Problem Solving • Reasoning

2. How many people were at the concert Friday and Saturday?

_______ people

People at the Concert	
Friday	
Saturday	
Sunday	

Each stands for 100 people.

Name ______________________ Date ____________

Identify Place Value

Write each number.

1.

Hundreds	Tens	Ones
4	9	1

400 + 90 + 1

491

2.

Hundreds	Tens	Ones
7	2	6

700 + 20 + 6

______

3. 400 + 40 + 5 ______

4. 300 + 80 + 6 ______

5. 700 + 7 ______

6. 3 + 10 + 600 ______

7. 50 + 7 + 900 ______

8. 800 + 80 + 8 ______

9. 600 + 4 ______

10. 90 + 9 ______

11. 500 + 40 + 8 ______

Problem Solving • Reasoning

12. Use the clues to find the missing number.
- 5 is the hundreds place.
- The ones digit is 2 less than the hundreds digit.
- The tens digit is triple the ones digit.

______ hundreds ______ tens ______ ones

Name ____________________ Date __________

Regroup Tens as Hundreds

Use a pencil and paper clip to spin the spinner.

1. Spin the spinner two times. Write both numbers. Find the sum. Take that many tens.

2. Regroup 10 tens as 1 hundred when you can.

3. Write the hundreds, tens, and ones you have. Write the number.

First Spin	Second Spin	Sum
9	4	13

Hundreds	Tens	Ones
1	3	0

130

First Spin	Second Spin	Sum
____	____	____

Hundreds	Tens	Ones

____

First Spin	Second Spin	Sum
____	____	____

Hundreds	Tens	Ones

____

First Spin	Second Spin	Sum
____	____	____

Hundreds	Tens	Ones

____

Name ______________________ Date ____________

Problem Solving: Make a Table

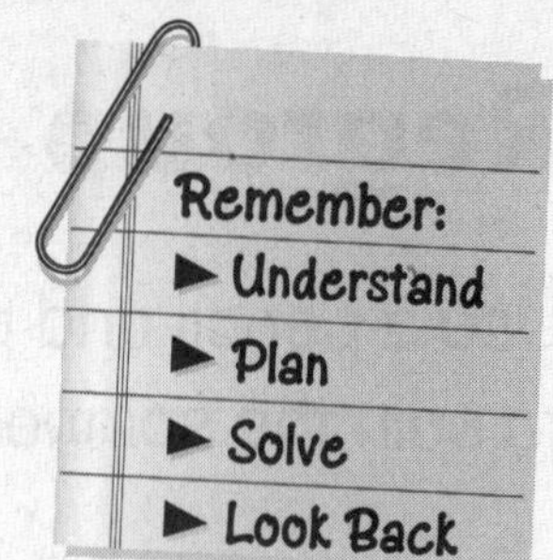

Sometimes you can make a table to help solve a problem.

Solve. Complete the table.

1. Carmen reads 8 chapters every night. How many chapters does she read in 4 nights?

Think: How many chapters each night?

Night	1	2	3	4
Chapters	8	16		

_____ chapters

2. The toy factory makes 20 teddy bears a day. How many teddy bears do they make in 5 days?

Think: What do I need to find out?

Day	1	2	3	4	5
Teddy Bears	20				

_____ teddy bears

Solve. Choose a strategy.

- Make a table.
- Guess and check.
- Write a number sentence.

3. Everyone at the party ate 2 tacos. If 18 tacos were eaten, how many people came to the party?

_____ people

Draw or write to explain.

Name ______________________ Date ____________

Different Ways to Show Numbers

Circle another way to show the number.

1. 526 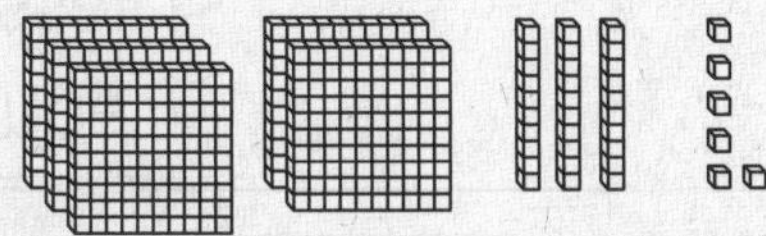 500 + 20 + 6

2. 716 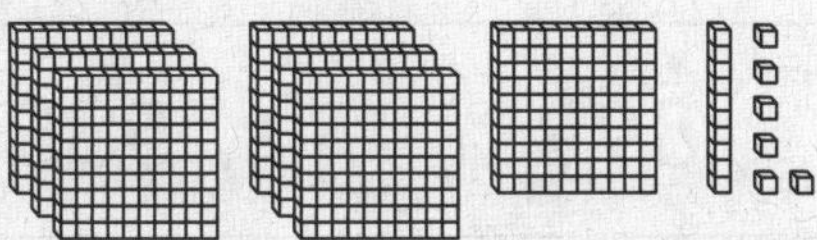 7 hundreds 6 tens 1 one

3. 289 200 + 90 + 8 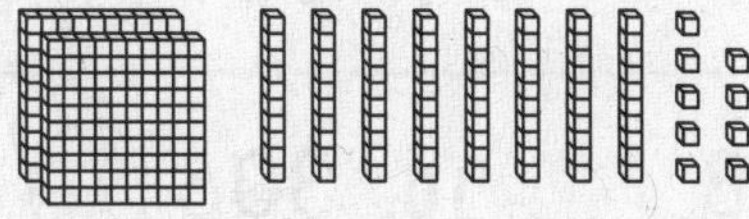

4. 307 3 hundreds 7 ones 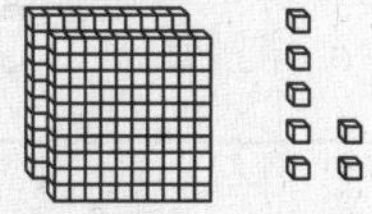

5. 477 4 hundreds 7 tens 7 ones 400 + 7 + 7

6. 852 8 hundreds 2 tens 5 ones 800 + 50 + 2

Problem Solving • Reasoning

7. Maria has three sheets with 100 fish each. She has two sheets with 10 fish each. She has one sheet with 9 more fish. How many fish does she have?

_____ fish

Draw or write to explain.

Name ______________________________ Date ______________

Compare Three-Digit Numbers

Compare the numbers.
Write >, <, or = in the ◯.

> greater than
< less than
= equals

1. 607 (<) 706
2. 354 ◯ 354

3. 255 ◯ 275
4. 999 ◯ 899
5. 535 ◯ 565

6. 671 ◯ 661
7. 809 ◯ 909
8. 365 ◯ 389

9. 788 ◯ 788
10. 306 ◯ 316
11. 156 ◯ 160

12. 412 ◯ 411
13. 509 ◯ 510
14. 273 ◯ 271

15. 301 ◯ 301
16. 839 ◯ 851
17. 111 ◯ 111

18. 221 ◯ 212
19. 454 ◯ 445
20. 726 ◯ 726

Problem Solving • Reasoning

21. Leroy drove 867 miles from Miami to Charleston. Deshawn drove 895 miles from Miami to New Orleans. Who drove farther?

____

22. Explain how you compared the numbers. ______________

Name ______________________ Date ____________

Before, After, Between

Write each number.

	Before	Between	After
1.	716, 717	718, 719, 720	724, 725
2.	____, 282	284, ____, 286	288, ____
3.	____, 678	681, ____, 683	687, ____
4.	____, 435	436, ____, 438	440, ____
5.	____, 205	207, ____, 209	211, ____

Write the missing numbers.

6. 965, ____, ____, 968, ____, 970, 971, ____, ____, ____

7. 333, ____, 335, ____, ____, 338, 339, ____, 341, ____

8. ____, 627, 628, ____, ____, 631, ____, 633, ____, ____

9. ____, 890, 891, ____, 893, ____, ____, ____, ____, 898

Problem Solving • Reasoning

10. Match the words to the correct sign.

equal to	greater than	less than

< = >

Name ______________________ Date ____________

Order Three-Digit Numbers

Order the numbers from **least** to **greatest.**

1. 252, 175, 109, 262 — 109, 175, 252, 262
2. 209, 310, 290, 309 — ____, ____, ____, ____
3. 210, 176, 219, 267 — ____, ____, ____, ____
4. 653, 682, 628, 699 — ____, ____, ____, ____
5. 412, 421, 521, 402 — ____, ____, ____, ____

Order the numbers from **greatest** to **least.**

6. 232, 291, 223, 323 — ____, ____, ____, ____
7. 490, 409, 904, 410 — ____, ____, ____, ____
8. 279, 272, 329, 293 — ____, ____, ____, ____
9. 888, 818, 928, 882 — ____, ____, ____, ____
10. 563, 536, 569, 573 — ____, ____, ____, ____

Problem Solving • Reasoning

11. Look at the picture of the runners. Put their numbers in order from **least** to **greatest.**

____, ____, ____, ____, ____

Name ______________________ Date __________

Count Dollars and Cents

Count to find the total amount.

1.   

2.  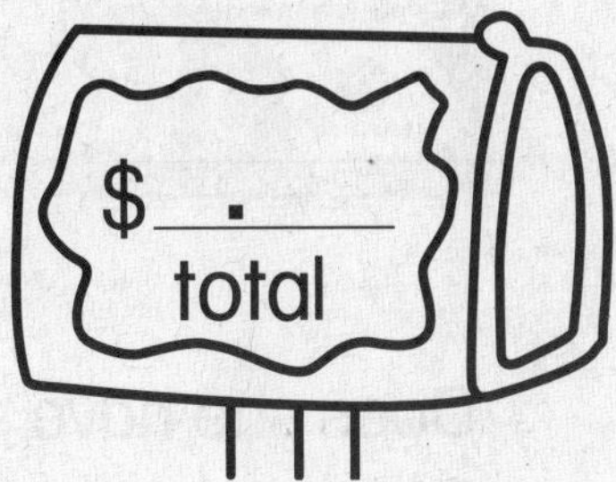

3.  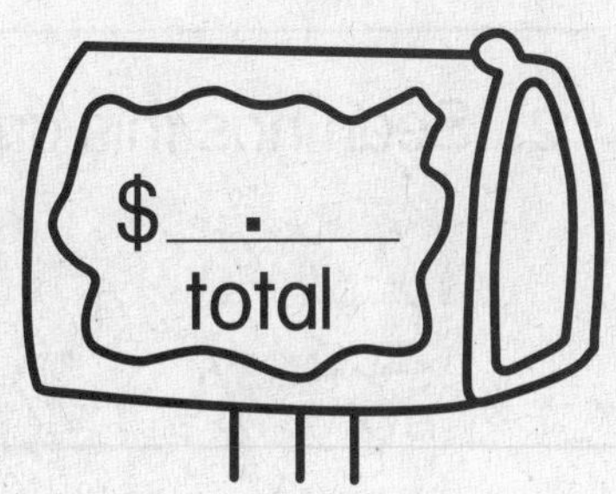

Problem Solving • Reasoning

Circle the correct way to show the amount.

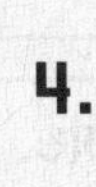

4. 

$6.03 $.63 $.36

Name ______________________ Date ____________

Problem Solving: Using Money

You can count bills and coins to find out if there is enough money.

$1.35

$1.90 ADMIT ONE

Write how much money. Decide if there is enough money. Write **yes** or **no.**

1. Irina has this amount. 

Think: How much money does she need?

Does she have enough to buy popcorn? ______
Circle the bills and coins she can use.

---

2. Sean has this amount. 

Think: How much money does he need?

Draw or write to explain.

Does he have enough to buy a movie ticket? ______
Draw the coins he needs.

Solve. Choose a strategy.

- Make a table.
- Draw a picture.

3. Latisha bought candy and paid for it with 2 quarters. How much change did she get? ______¢

Draw or write to explain.

Name ____________________ Date ____________

Mental Math: Add Hundreds

Add. Look for a pattern.

1. $\begin{array}{r} 3 \\ +3 \\ \hline 6 \end{array}$ $\begin{array}{r} 30 \\ +30 \\ \hline 60 \end{array}$ $\begin{array}{r} 300 \\ +300 \\ \hline 600 \end{array}$

2. $\begin{array}{r} 2 \\ +6 \\ \hline \end{array}$ $\begin{array}{r} 20 \\ +60 \\ \hline \end{array}$ $\begin{array}{r} 200 \\ +600 \\ \hline \end{array}$

3. $\begin{array}{r} 500 \\ +200 \\ \hline \end{array}$ $\begin{array}{r} 200 \\ +500 \\ \hline \end{array}$

4. $\begin{array}{r} 5 \\ +3 \\ \hline \end{array}$ $\begin{array}{r} 50 \\ +30 \\ \hline \end{array}$ $\begin{array}{r} 500 \\ +300 \\ \hline \end{array}$

5. $\begin{array}{r} 5 \\ +1 \\ \hline \end{array}$ $\begin{array}{r} 50 \\ +10 \\ \hline \end{array}$ $\begin{array}{r} 500 \\ +100 \\ \hline \end{array}$

6. $\begin{array}{r} 6 \\ +3 \\ \hline \end{array}$ $\begin{array}{r} 60 \\ +30 \\ \hline \end{array}$ $\begin{array}{r} 600 \\ +300 \\ \hline \end{array}$

7. $\begin{array}{r} 200 \\ +300 \\ \hline \end{array}$ $\begin{array}{r} 300 \\ +200 \\ \hline \end{array}$

8. $\begin{array}{r} 100 \\ +700 \\ \hline \end{array}$ $\begin{array}{r} 700 \\ +100 \\ \hline \end{array}$

Problem Solving • Reasoning

Follow the rule. Complete each table.

9.

Add 100	
500	
600	
700	
800	

10.

Add 200	
200	
300	
400	
500	

11.

Add 400	
200	
300	
400	
500	

Name ______________________ Date ____________

Regroup Ones

Add. Regroup 10 ones as 1 ten.

1.

	H	T	O
		1	
	1	2	8
+	4	1	7
	5	4	5

2.

	H	T	O
	5	6	3
+	2	0	9

3.

	H	T	O
	7	5	6
+	1	1	6

4. $\begin{array}{r} 438 \\ +126 \\ \hline \end{array}$

5. $\begin{array}{r} 304 \\ +315 \\ \hline \end{array}$

6. $\begin{array}{r} 223 \\ +348 \\ \hline \end{array}$

7. $\begin{array}{r} 754 \\ +209 \\ \hline \end{array}$

8. $\begin{array}{r} 815 \\ +143 \\ \hline \end{array}$

9. $\begin{array}{r} 627 \\ +218 \\ \hline \end{array}$

10. $\begin{array}{r} 543 \\ +326 \\ \hline \end{array}$

11. $\begin{array}{r} 185 \\ +406 \\ \hline \end{array}$

Problem Solving • Reasoning

12. Les has 124 baseball cards and 67 football cards. How many cards does he have in all?

_____ cards

Draw or write to explain.

Name ______________________ Date ____________

Regroup Tens

Add.

1.

	H	T	O
	1		
	1	2	6
+	4	9	2
	6	1	8

2.

	H	T	O
	☐		
	2	4	1
+	5	7	2

3.

	H	T	O
		☐	
	3	1	8
+	4	7	5

4. $328 + 67$

5. $195 + 221$

6. $784 + 25$

7. $463 + 194$

8. $628 + 49$

9. $892 + 74$

10. $375 + 184$

11. $208 + 316$

Problem Solving • Reasoning

12. A ticket to the ball game costs $1.45. Can Tia buy a ticket to the game? Tell why. ______________

Tia's Money

Name ______________________ Date __________

Mental Math: Subtract Hundreds

Subtract. Look for a pattern.

1. $\begin{array}{r} 8 \\ -2 \\ \hline 6 \end{array}$ $\begin{array}{r} 80 \\ -20 \\ \hline 60 \end{array}$ $\begin{array}{r} 800 \\ -200 \\ \hline 600 \end{array}$

2. $\begin{array}{r} 7 \\ -5 \\ \hline \end{array}$ $\begin{array}{r} 70 \\ -50 \\ \hline \end{array}$ $\begin{array}{r} 700 \\ -500 \\ \hline \end{array}$

3. $\begin{array}{r} 9 \\ -6 \\ \hline \end{array}$ $\begin{array}{r} 90 \\ -60 \\ \hline \end{array}$ $\begin{array}{r} 900 \\ -600 \\ \hline \end{array}$

4. $\begin{array}{r} 6 \\ -4 \\ \hline \end{array}$ $\begin{array}{r} 60 \\ -40 \\ \hline \end{array}$ $\begin{array}{r} 600 \\ -400 \\ \hline \end{array}$

5. $\begin{array}{r} 8 \\ -4 \\ \hline \end{array}$ $\begin{array}{r} 80 \\ -40 \\ \hline \end{array}$ $\begin{array}{r} 800 \\ -400 \\ \hline \end{array}$

6. $\begin{array}{r} 7 \\ -3 \\ \hline \end{array}$ $\begin{array}{r} 70 \\ -30 \\ \hline \end{array}$ $\begin{array}{r} 700 \\ -300 \\ \hline \end{array}$

7. $\begin{array}{r} 500 \\ -200 \\ \hline \end{array}$ $\begin{array}{r} 500 \\ -300 \\ \hline \end{array}$

8. $\begin{array}{r} 900 \\ -500 \\ \hline \end{array}$ $\begin{array}{r} 900 \\ -400 \\ \hline \end{array}$

Problem Solving • Reasoning

9. How many more rooms does the Rainbow Hotel have than the Sleep Inn?

_____ more rooms

Hotel Name	Number of Rooms
Rainbow Hotel	800
Cloud House	600
Sleep Inn	300

10. **Write Your Own** Use data from the table to write a subtraction problem. Then solve.

Name ______________________________ Date ______________

Regroup Tens

Subtract. Regroup 1 ten as 10 ones.

1.

	H	T	O
		8	14
	2	~~9~~	~~4~~
−	1	5	8
	1	3	6

2.

	H	T	O
		☐	☐
	6	5	7
−	4	2	9

3.

	H	T	O
		☐	☐
	7	8	4
−	3	5	6

4.

		☐	☐
	5	7	2
−	3	4	8

5.

		☐	☐
	7	2	3
−	2	1	5

6.

		☐	☐
	4	2	6
−	1	1	8

7. 566 − 248 = ____

8. 260 − 145 = ____

9. 893 − 587 = ____

10. 425 − 116 = ____

Problem Solving • Reasoning

11. Bob and Jane are walking on the path. They have 110 feet to go before they reach the end. How far have they walked already? _____ feet

Name ______________________ Date ____________

Regroup Hundreds

Subtract.

1.

	H	T	O
	4	11	
	5	1	6
−	2	7	3
	2	4	3

2.

	H	T	O
	9	2	7
−	7	5	1

3.

	H	T	O
	6	4	5
−	2	8	2

4. 898 − 269

5. 503 − 412

6. 650 − 225

7. 761 − 453

8. 194 − 85

9. 273 − 116

10. 619 − 384

11. 556 − 291

12. 417 − 162

13. 708 − 355

14. 624 − 361

15. 829 − 562

Problem Solving • Reasoning

16. You regroup a number and get 8 hundreds, 11 tens, and 6 ones. What number did you start with?

______

Draw or write to explain.

Name ______________________ Date ____________

Problem Solving: Choose the Operation

To decide whether to add or subtract, think about whether you need a larger or smaller number as an answer.

Circle the number sentence you would use. Then solve.

1. Pedro's team scored 116 points in their first game and 85 points in their second game. How many more points did they score in their first game?

   116 + 85 = ■

   116 − 85 = ■

   Think: I need to compare two numbers.

   ____ points

   Draw or write to explain.

2. The 8th grade had a bake sale. They sold 130 cookies in the morning and 200 cookies in the afternoon. How many cookies did they sell in all?

   200 − 130 = ■

   130 + 200 = ■

   Think: I need to find how many cookies sold in all.

   ____ cookies

   Draw or write to explain.

Solve. Choose a strategy.

- Make a table.
- Write a number sentence.

3. Every day, our class recycles 30 bottles. How many do we recycle in 6 days?

   ____ bottles

Name ______________________ Date ____________

Horizontal Addition and Subtraction

Add or subtract.

1. 485 − 192 3 18 ~~4~~ ~~8~~ 5 − 1 9 2 293	2. 197 + 241 +	3. 356 − 293 −	4. 273 + 118 +
5. 907 − 534 −	6. 215 + 677 +	7. 538 − 173 −	8. 415 + 269 +
9. 651 − 324 −	10. 311 + 279 +	11. 423 − 192 −	12. 564 + 173 +

13. How many cans were collected by children in Grades 1 and 2?

_____ cans

14. How many more cans did children in Grade 2 collect than children in Grade 3?

_____ more cans

Canned Food	
Grade	Cans Collected
1	347
2	429
3	284

Name ______________________ Date __________

Algebra Readiness: Check Subtraction

Subtract. Check by adding.

1. $\begin{array}{r} 416 \\ -293 \\ \hline 123 \end{array}$ $\begin{array}{r} 123 \\ +293 \\ \hline 416 \end{array}$

2. $\begin{array}{r} 589 \\ -215 \\ \hline \end{array}$ $+$

3. $\begin{array}{r} 516 \\ -475 \\ \hline \end{array}$ $+$

4. $\begin{array}{r} 624 \\ -281 \\ \hline \end{array}$ $+$

5. $\begin{array}{r} 826 \\ -492 \\ \hline \end{array}$ $+$

6. $\begin{array}{r} 746 \\ -455 \\ \hline \end{array}$ $+$

Problem Solving • Reasoning

Use these digits: 3, 4, 5, 6, 7.

7. Use all the digits. Make the greatest possible sum.

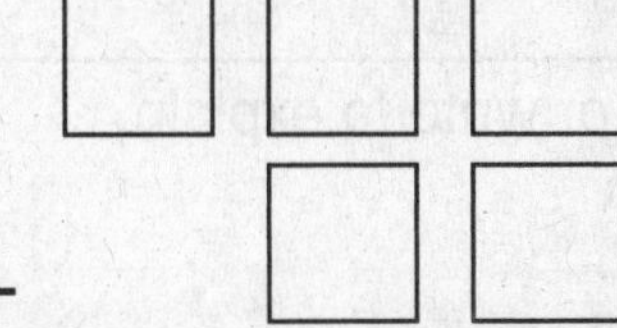

8. Use all the digits. Make the least possible sum.

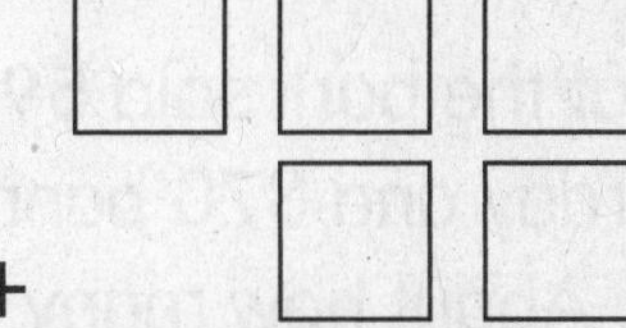

Name ________________________ Date ____________

Estimate Sums and Differences

Round each number to the nearest hundred.
Estimate the sum or difference.

1.
590 — nearest hundred → 600
−410 — nearest hundred → − 400

590 − 410 is about 200

2.
520 → ☐
−430 → − ☐

520 − 430 is about ____

3.
570 → ☐
−190 → − ☐

570 − 190 is about ____

4.
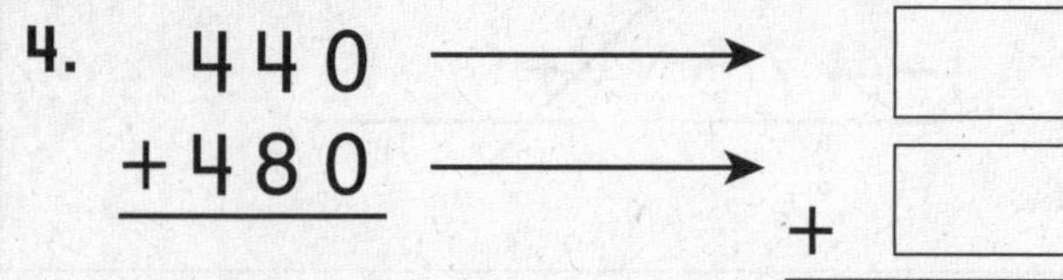
440 → ☐
+480 → + ☐

440 + 480 is about ____

5.
520 → ☐
+420 → + ☐

520 + 420 is about ____

6.
430 → ☐
+490 → + ☐

430 + 490 is about ____

400 410 420 430 440 450 460 470 480 490 **500** 510 520 530 540 550 560 570 580 590 **600**

Problem Solving • Reasoning

7. A shop at the park sold 590 banners on Saturday and 370 banners on Sunday. About how many fewer banners were sold on Sunday?

_____ fewer banners

Draw or write to explain.

Name ______________________ Date ____________

Add and Subtract Money

Add or subtract.

1. $5.62 +1.34 $6.96	2. $8.26 −4.15	3. $4.38 +1.45	4. $6.25 −3.70
5. $8.15 +1.71	6. $4.02 −2.50	7. $1.86 +2.05	8. $4.37 −1.15
9. $7.23 +2.45	10. $5.12 −3.71	11. $8.20 +1.45	12. $6.37 −5.19

Problem Solving • Reasoning

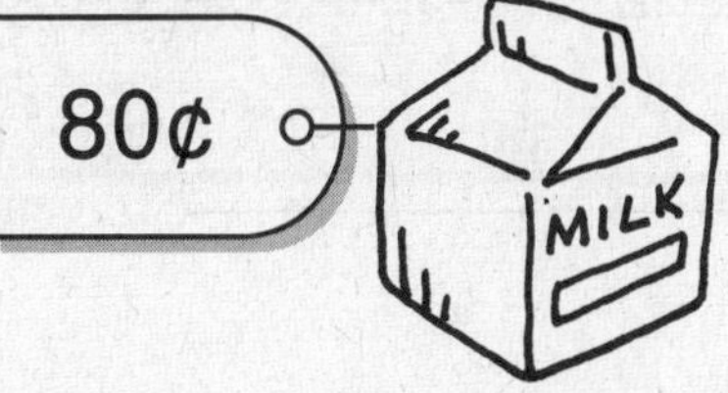

13. Van has $6.78. He buys a sandwich and milk for lunch. How much money does Van spend? __________

14. How much does Van have left? __________

Draw or write to explain.

Name ____________________ Date ____________

Problem Solving: Guess and Check

Remember:
- ► Understand
- ► Plan
- ► Solve
- ► Look Back

You can use the Guess and Check strategy to solve a problem.

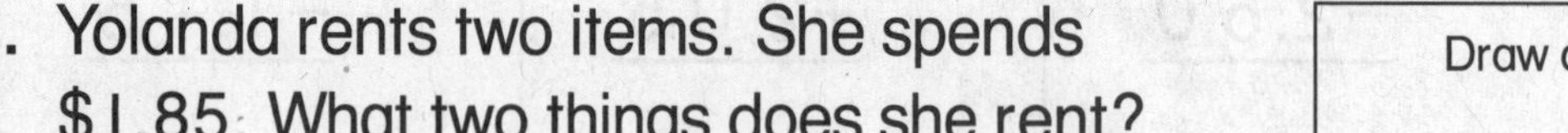

1. Yolanda rents two items. She spends $1.85. What two things does she rent?

____

____

Think: Which two things total $1.85?

Draw or write to explain.

---

2. Ari and his sister each rent the same thing. They spend $3.00.

____

Think: Two of which thing totals $3.00?

Draw or write to explain.

Solve. Choose a strategy.

- Guess and check.
- Use models to act it out.

3. Emma rents a pair of roller skates and knee pads. She pays with $2.00. How much change does she get?

______ ¢

Draw or write to explain.